WOMEN'S
RIGHTS

WOMEN'S 3
RIGHTS ꞁYA

GREAT
SPEECHES
IN
HISTORY

Jennifer A. Hurley, *Book Editor*

Daniel Leone, *Publisher*

Bonnie Szumski, *Editorial Director*

Scott Barbour, *Managing Editor*

Greenhaven Press, Inc.
San Diego, California

Every effort has been made to trace the owners of copyrighted material. The articles in this volume may have been edited for content, length, and/or reading level. The titles have been changed to enhance the editorial purpose.

No part of this book may be reproduced or used in any form or by any means, electrical, mechanical, or otherwise, including, but not limited to, photocopy, recording, or any information storage and retrieval system, without prior written permission from the publisher.

Library of Congress Cataloging-in-Publication Data

Women's rights / Jennifer A. Hurley, book editor.
p. cm. — (Great speeches in history)
Includes bibliographical references and index.
ISBN 0-7377-0772-0 (pbk. : alk. paper) —
ISBN 0-7377-0773-9 (lib. : alk. paper) —
1. Women's rights. 2. Women's rights—History—Sources. 3. Feminism. I. Hurley, Jennifer A., 1973–   II. Series.

HQ1236 .W6526 2001
305.42—dc21

2001018988
CIP

Cover Photo: © Underwood & Underwood/CORBIS

Library of Congress, 42, 74, 208

© 2002 by Greenhaven Press, Inc
PO Box 28909, San Diego, CA
92198–0990

Printed in the U.S.A.

Contents

Chapter 2: Voices from the Suffrage Movement

The Equal Rights Amendment, if passed, would eradicate such distinctions and mandate the equal treatment of women.

fundamental human rights such as the freedom of
religion and speech, as well as freedom from
violence.

was fully articulated to a mass audience in a way that was both logical and evocative. Julian Bond, a fellow participant in the civil rights movement and student of King's, states that

> King's dramatic 1963 "I Have a Dream" speech before the Lincoln Memorial cemented his place as first among equals in civil rights leadership; from this first televised mass meeting, an American audience saw and heard the unedited oratory of America's finest preacher, and for the first time, a mass white audience heard the undeniable justice of black demands.

Moreover, by helping people to understand the justice of the civil rights movement's demands, King's speech helped to transform the nation. In 1964, a year after the speech was delivered, President Lyndon B. Johnson signed the Civil Rights Act, which outlawed segregation in public facilities and discrimination in employment. In 1965, Congress passed the Voting Rights Act, which forbids restrictions, such as literacy tests, that were commonly used in the South to prevent blacks from voting. King's impact on the country's laws illustrates the power of speech to bring about real change.

Greenhaven Press's Great Speeches in History series offers students an opportunity to read and study some of the greatest speeches ever delivered before an audience. Each volume traces a specific historical era, event, or theme through speeches—both famous and lesser known. An introductory essay sets the stage by presenting background and context. Then a collection of speeches follows, grouped in chapters based on chronology or theme. Each selection is preceded by a brief introduction that offers historical context, biographical information about the speaker, and analysis of the speech. A comprehensive index and an annotated table of contents help readers quickly locate material of interest, and a bibliography serves as a launching point for further research. Finally, an appendix of author biographies provides detailed background on each speaker's life and work. Taken together, the volumes in the Greenhaven Great Speeches in History series offer students vibrant illustrations of history and demonstrate the potency of the spoken word. By reading speeches in their historical context, students will be transported back in time and gain a deeper understanding of the issues that confronted people of the past.

Introduction

In 1840 a group of abolitionists from around the globe gathered in London for the World Anti-Slavery Convention. Several female delegates from the United States sailed across the Atlantic Ocean to attend the convention. However, on the first day of the proceedings, a number of male delegates argued that women should not be allowed to serve as delegates. Other men defended women's right to participate. A furious debate ensued among the men while the women, who were given no opportunity to speak, sat and listened. Eventually, the British Foreign Anti-Slavery Society, the organizing authority, voted to bar women from participation in the convention. Women could remain present, it stated, but must sit behind a galley curtain, where they could neither be seen nor heard.

Female delegates from the United States, who were accustomed to speaking in public arenas (although they still experienced discrimination within American anti-slavery organizations), felt humiliated by the decision. However, the convention provided women with a valuable opportunity to share ideas and form coalitions. It was there that Lucretia Mott and Elizabeth Cady Stanton—who would become two of the most prominent women's rights activists—met and vowed to hold their own convention back in the States to address the concerns of women.

This convention would not take place until eight years later, in July 1848, when Mott, Stanton, and three other friends gathered in New York for a social visit. During an afternoon tea, Stanton spoke passionately about her frustration with the restrictions on women's freedoms. She proposed a convention to "discuss the social, civil, and religious condition and rights of women." Although women's rights had been a topic of discussion since 1792, when British writer Mary Wollstonecraft published the feminist treatise *A Vindication of the Rights of Woman*, never before had a group of women held a public forum whose specific purpose was to demand women's social and political rights.

The Seneca Falls Convention

The women who organized the Seneca Falls women's rights convention were fervent patriots who respected the lofty ideals of the founding fathers. Thus, Elizabeth Cady Stanton used the Declaration of Independence as the model for her "Declaration of Sentiments," a document enumerating the ways that women were treated unjustly. She listed eighteen grievances, precisely the number of grievances the revolutionaries had listed in their Declaration of Independence from England. As stated by the National Women's History Project, women's grievances included the following:

- Married women were legally dead in the eyes of the law.
- Women were not allowed to vote.
- Women had to submit to laws when they had no voice in their formation.
- Married women had no property rights.
- Husbands had legal power over and responsibility for their wives to the extent that they could imprison or beat them with impunity.
- Divorce and child custody laws favored men, giving no rights to women.
- Women had to pay property taxes although they had no representation in the levying of these taxes.
- Most occupations were closed to women, and when women did work, they were paid only a fraction of what men earned.
- Women were not allowed to enter professions such as medicine or law.
- Women had no means to gain an education since no college or university would accept female students.

- With only a few exceptions, women were not allowed to participate in the affairs of the church.
- Women were robbed of their self-confidence and self-respect and were made totally dependent on men.

The first women's rights convention was hastily organized within only a few days; a flyer published in the local newspaper was its only publicity. However, on July 19, 1848, the first day of the convention, over three hundred women and forty men arrived at the Wesleyan Chapel in Seneca Falls, New York. Stanton read the Declaration of Sentiments and asked the attendees to give their approval to twelve resolutions aimed at remedying women's grievances. Each of these passed unanimously except for the resolution for women's suffrage. At the time, the idea that women should be allowed to vote was extremely controversial. When Stanton had first proposed that convention leaders include suffrage in their list of demands, Lucretia Mott had exclaimed, "Why, Lizzie, thee will make us ridiculous!"

Viewed from a modern perspective, the widespread opposition to women's suffrage—especially among women's rights activists—is difficult to fathom. However, as historian Ellen DuBois explains, women's suffrage was regarded as radical because it "called for a new kind of power for women not based in the family; a nonfamilial role for women in the public sphere challenged the male monopoly on the public arena." Women themselves often felt threatened by the notion that their well-defined role might change.

Stanton implored those present at the convention to accept the resolution for women's suffrage, but she was unable to persuade them. She then appealed to Frederick Douglass, an eminent abolitionist who was well known for his eloquence as a speaker. Douglass passionately voiced his support for suffrage, insisting that, as historian Doris Weatherford writes, "without this fundamental right to participate in government, the principle of equality for women would never be taken seriously." Douglass's speech helped the suffrage resolution to pass by a slim margin. At the convention's end, one hundred people signed their names to the Declaration of Sentiments. Sadly, only one of these signers, glovemaker Charlotte Woodward, would live to cast a legal ballot.

Reaction to the Convention

The convention at Seneca Falls provoked a torrent of sarcasm and ridicule from the press. This only pleased Stanton. When the *New York Herald* printed the entire Declaration of Sentiments in order to mock it, Stanton said that it was "just what I wanted. Imagine the publicity given to our ideas by thus appearing in a widely circulated sheet like the *Herald*. It will start women thinking, and men, too; and when men and women think about a new question, the first step in progress is taken."

Her prediction proved correct. The publicity gained from the press's criticism helped turn a small uprising into a large-scale movement. What the first women's rights leaders hoped for—"a series of conventions embracing every part of the country"—soon became a reality. From 1850 until the start of the Civil War in 1861, women's rights conventions were held regularly in locations all over the country. Due to these conventions, women accomplished many of their goals, such as winning women property rights and greater access to education.

Winning the right to vote, on the other hand, seemed an insurmountable task. Yet women's rights leaders eventually recognized suffrage as the essential objective of the women's rights movement. Without having a voice in government, suffragists argued, women could never achieve true equality.

The Fight for Suffrage

Just as support for suffrage was mounting, the onset of the Civil War in 1861 brought an abrupt end to the movement, as suffragists—the vast majority of whom were also abolitionists—shelved their cause to support the war effort. From 1861 to 1865, no women's rights conventions were held; instead, female activists devoted themselves to nursing, fundraising, and relief work.

Shortly after the South surrendered in the spring of 1865, Congress began to discuss the passage of the Fourteenth Amendment, which was designed to give freed slaves the right to vote. Unfortunately, the proposed amendment specifically excluded women. In fact, the amendment blatantly prohibited women's suffrage by introducing the word *male* into the U.S. Constitution. Stanton and Susan B. Anthony, who were both supporters of black suffrage, launched a campaign against the Fourteenth Amendment on the basis of its gender-specific language. Thus began a bitter conflict between abolitionists and suffragists, who had previously been close allies. Abolitionists argued that women's suffrage should be put on hold until black men won the right to vote, meanwhile many suffragist leaders were opposed to any measure that did not enfranchise both groups.

Despite suffragists' attempts to modify the Fourteenth Amendment, it passed as it was originally written in July 1868. A few months later, a Fifteenth Amendment was introduced into Congress, stating that the right to vote could not be denied "on account of race, color, or previous condition of servitude." This time, controversy erupted within the suffrage movement. Stanton and Anthony stated that they could not support an amendment unless the word *sex* were added to it, but other suffragists—led by Lucy Stone—argued that it was their moral duty to support any law that protected the enfranchisement of black men.

The conflict split the suffrage movement into two distinct factions. In 1869 Stanton and Anthony organized the National Women's Suffrage Association (NWSA), whose principal aim was the passage of a national amendment granting women's suffrage. NWSA also promoted contentious causes such as women's labor unions and liberal divorce laws. A few months later Stone founded the American Women's Suffrage Association (AWSA), whose strategy was to win suffrage state by state. In contrast to the NWSA, whose philosophy and methods were radical, the AWSA appealed to the mainstream. Interestingly, during this ideological battle between the two suffrage organizations, the legislature of the Wyoming Territory passed a law granting women the right to vote—the first real victory for the suffrage movement.

In keeping with its revolutionary spirit, the NWSA then instigated a new tactic. Arguing that the Constitution actually upheld women's right to vote, some women ventured to exercise this right. In 1871 and 1872, approximately 150 women attempted to vote in ten states and the District of Columbia.

Susan B. Anthony was among the women who tried to vote in the 1872 presidential election. She persuaded election officials in Rochester, New York, to allow her and twelve female friends to cast ballots. Two weeks later, the women and election officials were arrested. Anthony was found guilty and was fined, but she refused to pay the penalty.

Virginia Minor, another woman who had attempted to vote in the 1872 presidential election, sued the official who had refused to allow her to register. Her case reached the Supreme Court, but with disappointing results: The justices ruled unanimously that the Constitution did not guarantee the right of all citizens to vote.

The Movement Reunites

Minor's defeat in court was followed by a series of other defeats for the suffragists. The AWSA's vigorous state-by-state campaign to enfranchise women was proving ineffectual: From 1870 to 1910, only four states would grant women the right to vote. The NWSA was equally unproductive in its quest for a federal women's suffrage amendment. Although supporters introduced such an amendment in every session of Congress since 1868, the measure usually failed to make it past initial committee hearings.

The two organizations eventually agreed that a united effort was essential to the success of suffrage. Consequently, in 1890 the movement reunited as the National American Women's Suffrage Association (NAWSA). The new organization concentrated solely on women's suffrage and divided its energies between state and federal campaigns. Unfortunately, between 1890 and 1910, the movement experienced a period that is referred to as "the doldrums." Suffragists expended a vast amount of energy, but nothing concrete was achieved. Many women who had grown gray fighting for the cause began to question whether suffrage would ever be won.

However, in the decade following the doldrums, the movement made rapid strides. In 1910 Washington State passed a law granting women's suffrage; two years later, California did the same. Then, in 1913, the U.S. Senate held discussions on suffrage for the first time. Although the amendment failed to win the necessary two-thirds majority, the Senate vote revitalized the suffrage movement. From that point on, the suffragists launched a vigorous and incessant campaign, aggressively lobbying the support of legislators. Women picketed the White House, enduring harsh weather conditions and the assault of hecklers. Many were arrested and went on hunger strikes during their time in prison.

On January 9, 1918, President Woodrow Wilson formally gave his endorsement to women's suffrage. A year later both houses of Congress approved a federal amendment enfranchising women. Because the nation's mood was largely pro-suffrage, ratification by the states was obtained relatively quickly—within fifteen months. On August 26, 1920, the Nineteenth Amendment was signed into law, and in the November elections of that year, millions of women voted for the first time.

A Period of Dormancy

Most women's rights leaders regarded suffrage as only the first step—albeit a crucial one—to achieving women's equality. However, having devoted more than seventy years of struggle to win suffrage, women's rights leaders were conflicted over what their new agenda should be. Alice Paul, founder of the National Women's Party, drafted an Equal Rights Amendment (ERA) in 1923 with the intention of making sex discrimination unconstitutional. Paul and others argued that the law would ensure that "men and women have equal rights throughout the United States." However, many former suffragists refused to support the ERA for fear that it would remove legal protections for women workers. As a result of internal conflicts such as this one, the movement splintered into different factions and lost momentum as a whole.

One of these factions was the birth control movement. Instigated by Margaret Sanger, a nurse who had watched hundreds of women die painful deaths during labor, the movement fought for access to contraception. At that time birth control was unavailable to all but the extremely wealthy, and the only legal use of contraception was condoms to protect men from venereal disease while having sex with prostitutes. Sanger argued that all women had the right to decide whether to have a child and should therefore have access to birth control. In an attempt to make birth control available to women of the lower classes, she opened the first birth control clinic in 1916. Soon afterward the clinic was raided by the police and Sanger was arrested. After her release, however, she continued to distribute family-planning materials to the poor.

Aside from Sanger's crusade for greater access to birth control, the women's rights movement was essentially dormant from roughly the 1920s until the beginning of the 1960s. The Great Depression and World War II were major factors contributing to this dormancy. Furthermore, the postwar culture of the 1950s favored a highly traditional lifestyle in which men had careers and women stayed at home to raise children.

"The Problem That Has No Name"

Although popular television shows advanced the image of the happy housewife, in reality many housewives of the 1950s were dissatisfied with their daily routine of cleaning, cooking, and child care. One such housewife was Betty Friedan, a graduate of Smith College and the mother of two children. Wondering whether she was alone in her feelings of discontent, she sent a questionnaire to other Smith alumnae. Their responses revealed that the problem—which Friedan dubbed "the problem that has no name"—was widespread.

In 1963 Friedan published *The Feminine Mystique*, her study of suburban women's discontent. In the book Friedan argued that society "does not permit women to accept or gratify their basic need to grow and fulfill their potentialities as human beings." She called the suburban American home "a comfortable concentration camp" because it restricted women's lives so severely. *The Feminine Mystique*, which quickly became an international best-seller, acted as the primary catalyst of the second wave of the women's rights movement. Soon, middle-class suburban women across the country were organizing to discuss the problems they faced as individuals and as a group.

The liberal spirit of the 1960s also galvanized the women's

rights movement. First of all, the civil rights movement, which strove to improve the status of blacks in society, provoked many women to question their own status. Second, many women who had joined activist movements experienced discrimination on the basis of gender. Just as women within the nineteenth century anti-slavery movement had been forbidden to speak in public, many female activists of the 1960s were delegated to "support roles" within the civil rights and antiwar organizations. Consequently, many women branched off and formed their own movement.

The Second Wave

The second wave of women's rights encapsulated a diverse array of goals, ideas, and strategies; its members included middle-class housewives, single working women, and young college students. In general, the movement consisted of two camps. The first was the women's rights movement, which emphasized the need for legal reforms. The National Organization for Women (NOW), founded by Friedan in 1966, was the principal women's rights group. Its goals were to bring women into full participation in the mainstream of American society; to eradicate discrimination against women in the workplace, politics, and law; and to challenge the traditional roles of men as breadwinners and women as homemakers.

Employment discrimination was NOW's main issue. In 1960 women earned only sixty cents for every dollar earned by men. Moreover, employment advertisements were typically segregated by gender, with high-paying, creative positions reserved for men and low-paying, tedious jobs relegated to women. NOW's lobbying efforts eventually led to laws forbidding sex discrimination within the work world.

The second faction of the 1960s movement was the women's liberation movement. A grassroots movement comprising college students and young civil rights activists, women's liberation sought revolutionary change in the society's attitudes about women. Arguing that "the personal is political," liberationists strove to change norms guiding domestic life and sexuality. Social critics Alexander Bloom and Wini Brienes explain how women's liberation developed:

Through the vehicle of consciousness-raising groups, in which small groups of women shared personal experiences and recognized the common political and social sources of their problems, feminism spread. Housework, sexuality, sexual orientation, relationships, mothering, day care, and work became topics analyzed from the perspective of women. The conclusions drawn were that American society was patriarchal and sexist, depended upon women's labor and love, and yet denigrated not only their activities but women themselves.

The women's liberation movement quickly earned publicity for its confrontational tactics. For example, at the Miss America contest in 1968, the New York Radical Women crowned a live sheep Miss America to illustrate their view that beauty pageant contestants were "judged like animals at a county fair." They also filled a "freedom trash can" with copies of fashion magazines, high-heeled shoes, hair curlers, and brassieres—items that they felt represented women's societal role as sex objects. A false rumor that the trash can was set on fire led to the rampant stereotype that women libbers (as they often called themselves) were "bra burners."

During the 1970s the two factions of the women's rights movement merged, as NOW began to adopt a more radical platform that included lesbian rights. Many of the radical liberationists joined with the more conservative middle-class suburban housewives in hopes that a unified movement would be more powerful. These women engaged in a wide variety of projects, such as the development of women's newspapers, battered women's shelters, child care centers, and health care clinics that dealt specifically with birth control and abortion.

In a departure from early women's rights leaders, who saw abortion as both immoral and harmful to women, most second-wave advocates regarded abortion rights as an important aspect of women's equality. Feminists argued that the right to choose when and if to have children was essential to women's liberty and autonomy. Therefore, the 1973 U.S. Supreme Court decision of *Roe v. Wade*, which legalized abortion, was considered a major feminist victory.

Evaluating the Second Wave

The effects of the second wave of the women's rights movement are still the subject of extensive debate. Most people agree that the movement benefited women by helping to pass laws prohibiting workplace discrimination and sexual harassment and by granting women access to credit and pension rights. As a direct result of such laws, the number of women holding political office, owning businesses, and working in professional positions has skyrocketed. The percentage of female legislators worldwide, for example, nearly doubled between the years 1975 and 1995.

However, some commentators argue that the movement was not entirely a success. For one, it failed to achieve one of its major goals: the enactment of an equal rights amendment. Introduced in every session of Congress beginning in 1923, the amendment finally passed in 1972 but was not ratified by the necessary thirty-eight states by the 1982 deadline. Since then, the amendment has lost widespread support.

Moreover, many argue that women are still getting paid less than men for the same job—seventy-four cents to the dollar—and still shoulder more than their share of domestic responsibilities. In fact, some maintain that the expansion of women's career opportunities created a society in which women must work twice as hard. Some contemporary women writers and speakers, collectively referred to as "postfeminists," contend that women should reinstitute homemaking and child care as their greatest priorities. Feminists, on the other hand, suggest that the workplace must be reformed so that both women and men can balance careers and home life.

Contemporary Women's Rights Activism

During the early 1980s feminism began to experience a dramatic backlash. A conservative-minded public tended to regard feminists as strident man haters, which led many women to detach themselves from the movement. Although feminism as a movement has largely moved out of the public eye since the mid-1970s, contemporary feminists have continued to fight discrimination against women in the military, sexual harassment, and violence against women.

One important aspect of the contemporary movement is global activism. Although women's rights was never limited to the United States—women in France, Britain, Australia, and Mexico also fought for suffrage in their respective countries—it was not until the 1960s that women from around the globe began to join forces to deal with international issues affecting women. Since that time groups of women have held conferences to voice their opposition to the persecution of women within developing countries. For example, in Afghanistan women are required by law to wear a shroud that covers their entire body and face, and they are not permitted to work or receive an education. In some Muslim societies women cannot have a job, own property, or even drive a car without their husband's permission; in Africa many women are subject to the brutal ritual of genital mutilation. The women's rights movement, in conjunction with human rights campaigns, has been active in criticizing these egregious practices.

The history of the women's rights movement—particularly its seventy-year-long crusade for suffrage—proves that women's perseverance will ultimately bring their goals to fruition. As the famous anthropologist Margaret Mead once wrote, "Never doubt that a small group of thoughtful, committed citizens can change the world; indeed, it is the only thing that ever has."

GREAT
SPEECHES
IN
HISTORY

Pioneers of the Women's Rights Movement

In Defense of Women's Rights

Elizabeth Cady Stanton

Elizabeth Cady Stanton's idea for a women's rights convention was born in 1840, when she met Quaker preacher Lucretia Mott in London at the World Anti-Slavery Convention, which refused to accept women as delegates. Stanton and Mott, both of whom had encountered discrimination within the predominantly male anti-slavery movement, agreed to address the condition of women at their own convention back in the States.

The convention would not occur until 1848, when a social visit brought Stanton, Mott, and several other women together in Seneca Falls, New York. Stanton suggested a convention be called "to discuss the social, civil, and religious condition and rights of women." She drafted a Declaration of Sentiments to be presented at the meeting, a document that was closely modeled on the Declaration of Independence and asserted that "all men and women are created equal." Among the convention's resolutions was the demand for universal suffrage—a demand considered so audacious that Mott exclaimed upon reading it, "Why, Lizzie, thee will make us ridiculous!"

Publicized only by a small notice placed in the *Seneca County Courier,* the convention drew close to three hundred people, including forty men. One of the attendants was Frederick Douglass, a former slave who had become an eloquent proponent of abolition. Douglass's talent as an orator was instrumental in persuading the audience to accept Stanton's resolution to obtain women's suffrage.

In this excerpt from her address to the Seneca Falls

From Elizabeth Cady Stanton's speech delivered at the Seneca Falls, New York, Convention, July 19, 1848.

Convention, Stanton refutes claims that men are intellectually, morally, and physically superior to women. She argues that women are equal to men and thus deserving of
equal rights. One of the most famous speeches in the history of the women's movement, the address to the Seneca
Falls Convention marks the beginning of Stanton's long
career as a renowned orator for women's rights.

A mong the many important questions which have been
brought before the public, there is none that more vi-
tally affects the whole human family than that which
is technically called Woman's Rights. Every allusion to the
degraded and inferior position occupied by women all over
the world has been met by scorn and abuse. From the man of
highest mental cultivation to the most degraded wretch who
staggers in the streets do we meet ridicule, and coarse jests,
freely bestowed upon those who dare assert that woman
stands by the side of man, his equal, placed here by her God,
to enjoy with him the beautiful earth, which is her home as
it is his, having the same sense of right and wrong, and looking to the same Being for guidance and support. So long has
man exercised tyranny over her, injurious to himself and be-
numbing to her faculties, that few can nerve themselves to
meet the storm; and so long has the chain been about her that
she knows not there is a remedy.

The whole social, civil and religious condition of woman
is a subject too vast to be brought within the limits of one short
lecture. Suffice it to say, for the present, wherever we turn, the
history of woman is sad and dark, without any alleviating circumstances, nothing from which we can draw consolation.

As the nations of the earth emerge from a state of bar-
barism, the sphere of woman gradually becomes wider, but
not even under what is thought to be the full blaze of the sun
of civilization is it what God designed it to be. In every country and clime does man assume the responsibility of marking
out the path for her to tread. In every country does he regard
her as a being inferior to himself, and one whom he is to guide
and control. From the Arabian Kerek, whose wife is obliged

to steal from her husband to supply the necessities of life; from the Mahometan [*sic*] who forbids pigs, dogs, women, and other impure animals, to enter a Mosque, and does not allow a fool, madman or woman to proclaim the hour of prayer; from the German who complacently smokes his meerschaum, while his wife, yoked with the ox, draws the plough through its furrow; from the delectable carpet-knight, who thinks an inferior style of conversation adapted to woman, to the legislator, who considers her incapable of saying what laws shall govern her, is the same feeling manifested. . . .

There is a class of men who believe in their natural, in-born, inbred superiority, and their heaven-descended right to dominion over the fish of the sea, the fowl of the air, and last, though not least, the immortal being called woman. I would recommend this class to the attentive perusal of their Bibles— Gen. 1:27; to historical research, to foreign travel, to a closer observation of the manifestations of mind about them, and to a humble comparison of themselves with such women as Catharine of Russia,[1] Elizabeth of England,[2] distinguished for their statesmanlike qualities; Harriet Martineau[3] and Madame De Staël,[4] for their literary attainments; or Caroline Herschel[5] and Mary Somerville[6] for their scientific researches; or for physical equality, to that whole nation of famous women, the Amazons. We seldom find this class of objectors among liberally educated persons, who have the advantage of observing the race in different countries, climes and phases. But barbarians though they be, in entertaining such an opinion, they must be met and fairly vanquished. Let us consider, then, man's superiority, intellectually, morally, physically.

Man's intellectual superiority cannot be a question until woman has had a fair trial. When we shall have had our freedom to find out our own sphere, when we shall have had our colleges, our professions, our trades, for a century, a comparison then may be justly instituted. When woman, instead of being taxed to endow colleges where she is forbidden to enter—instead of forming sewing societies to educate "poor, but pious," young men, shall first educate herself, when she shall be just to herself before she is generous to others; improving the talents God has given her, and leaving her neighbor to do the same for himself, we shall not then hear so much about this boasted superiority. How often, now, we see young men carelessly throwing away the intellectual food their sisters crave. A little music, that she may while an hour away pleasantly, a little French, a smattering of the sciences, and in rare instances, some slight classical knowledge, and woman is considered highly educated. She leaves her books and studies just as a young man is entering thoroughly into his. Then comes the gay routine of fashionable life, courtship and marriage, the perplexities of house and children, and she knows nothing beside. Her sphere is home. And whatever yearning her spirit may have felt for a higher existence, whatever may have been the capacity she well knew she possessed for more elevated enjoyments, enjoyments which would not conflict with those holy duties, but add new lustre to them, all, all is buried beneath the weight of these undivided cares.

Men, bless their innocence, are fond of representing themselves as beings of reason, of intellect, while women are mere creatures of the affections. There is a self-conceit that makes the possessor infinitely happy, and we would dislike to dispel the illusion if it were possible to endure it. But so far as we can observe, it is pretty much now-a-days as it was with Adam of old. No doubt you all recollect the account we have given us. A man and a woman were placed in a beautiful garden, with everything about them that could contribute to their enjoyment. Trees and shrubs, fruits and flowers, and gently murmuring streams made glad their hearts. Zephyrs freighted with delicious odors fanned their brows, and the serene stars looked down upon them with eyes of love. The Evil One saw their happiness, and it troubled him, and he set his wits to work to know how he should destroy it. He thought that man could be easily conquered through his affection for the woman, but the woman would require more management, she could be reached only through her intellectual nature. So he promised her the knowledge of good and evil. He told her the sphere of her reason should be enlarged. He promised to gratify the desires she felt for intellectual improvement. So he prevailed and she did eat. Did the Evil One judge rightly in regard to man? Eve took the apple, went to Adam, and said, "Dear Adam, taste this apple. If you love me, eat?" Adam stopped not so much as to ask if the apple were sweet or sour. He knew he was doing wrong, but his love for Eve prevailed, and he did eat. Which, I ask you, was the creature of the affections?

In consideration of man's claim to moral superiority, glance now at our theological seminaries, our divinity students, the long line of descendants from our Apostolic fathers, the immaculate priesthood, and what do we find here? Perfect moral rectitude in every relation of life, a devoted spirit of self-sacrifice, a perfect union of thought, opinion and feeling among those who profess to worship the one God, and whose laws they feel themselves called upon to declare to a fallen race? Far from it. These persons, all so thoroughly acquainted with the character of God, and of His designs, made manifest by His words and works, are greatly divided among themselves. Every sect has its God, every sect has its Bible, and there is as much bitterness, envy, hatred and malice between those contending sects, yea, even more, than in our political parties during the periods of their greatest excitement. Now the leaders of these sects are the priesthood, who are supposed to have passed their lives, almost, in the study of the Bible, in various languages and with various commentaries—in the contemplation of the infinite, the eternal, the glorious future open to the redeemed of earth. Are they distinguished among men for their holy aspirations, their virtue, purity and chastity? Do they keep themselves unspotted from the world? Is the moral and religious life of this class what we might expect from minds said to be fixed on such mighty themes? By no means. Not a year passes but we hear of some sad, soul-sickening deed, perpetrated by some of this class. If such be the state of the most holy, we need not pause now to consider those classes who claim of us less reverence and respect. The lamentable want of principle among our lawyers, generally, is too well known to need comment. The everlasting backbiting and bickering of our physicians is proverbial. The disgraceful riots at our polls, where man, in performing the highest duty of citizenship, and ought surely to be sober-minded, the perfect rowdyism that now characterizes the debates in our national Congress—all these are great facts which rise up against man's claim for moral superiority. In my opinion, he is infinitely woman's inferior in every moral quality, not by nature, but made so by a false education. In carrying out his own selfishness, man has greatly improved woman's moral nature, but by an almost total shipwreck of his own. Woman has now the noble virtues of the martyr. She is early schooled to self-denial and suffering. But man is not so wholly buried in selfishness that he does not sometimes get a glimpse of the narrowness of his soul, as compared with woman. Then he says, by way of an excuse for his degradation, "God made woman more self-denying than man. It is her nature. It does not cost her as much to give up her wishes, her will, her life, even, as it does him. He is naturally selfish. God made him so."

No! think not that He who made the heavens and the earth, the whole planetary world, ever moving in such harmony and order, that He who so bountifully scattered through all nature so much that fills us with admiration and wonder, that He who made the mighty ocean, mountain and cataract, the bright birds and tender flowers, that He who made man in his own image, perfect, noble and pure, loving justice, mercy and truth—oh say not that He has had any part in the production of that creeping, cringing, crawling, debased, selfish monster, now extant, claiming for himself the name of man. No! God's commands rest upon man as well as woman. It is as much his duty to be kind, self-denying and full of good works, as it is hers. As much his duty to absent himself from scenes of violence as it is hers. A place or position that would require the sacrifice of the delicacy and refinement of woman's nature is unfit for man, for these virtues should be as carefully guarded in him as in her. The false ideas that prevail with regard to the purity necessary to constitute the perfect character in woman, and that requisite for man, has done an infinite deal of mischief in the world. I would not have woman less pure, but I would have man more so. I would have the same code of morals for both. Delinquencies which exclude woman from the society of the true and the good, should assign to man the same place. Our laxity towards him has been the fruitful source of dissipation, drunkenness, debauchery and immorality of all kinds. It has not only affected woman injuriously, but he himself has been the greatest sufferer. It has destroyed the nobility of his char-

acter, the transparency of his soul, and all those finer qualities of our nature which raise us above the earth and give us
a foretaste of the refined enjoyments of the world to come.

Let us now consider man's claim to physical superiority.
Methinks I hear some say, surely, you will not contend for
equality here. Yes, we must not give an inch, lest you take an
ell. We cannot accord to man even this much, and he has no
right to claim it until the fact has been fully demonstrated.
Until the physical education of the boy and the girl shall have
been the same for many years. If you claim the advantage of
size, merely, why, it may be that under any course of training,
in ever so perfect a development of physique in woman, man
might still be the larger of the two, though we do not grant
even this. But the perfection of the physique is great power
combined with endurance. Now your strongest men are not
always the tallest men, nor the broadest, nor the most corpu-
lent, but very often the small, elastic man, who is well built,
tightly put together, and possessed of an indomitable will.
Bodily strength depends much on the power of the will. The
sight of a small boy thoroughly thrashing a big one, is not
rare. Now, would you say the big, fat boy whipped, was superior to the small active boy who conquered him? You do
not say the horse is physically superior to man, for although
he has more muscular power, yet the power of mind in man
renders him his superior, and he guides him wherever he will.
The power of mind seems to be in no way connected with the
size and strength of body. Many men of herculean powers of
mind have been small and weak in body. The late distinguished Dr. Channing,[7] of Boston, was feeble in appearance
and voice, yet he has moved the world by the eloquence of his
pen. John Quincy Adams was a small man of little muscular
power, yet we know he had more courage than all the Northern doughfaces, six feet high and well proportioned, that ever
represented us at our capitol. Mental power depends far more
on the temperament, than on the size of the head or the size
of the body. I never heard that Daniel Lambert was distinguished for any great mental achievements.[8] We cannot say
what the woman might be physically, if the girl were allowed
all the freedom of the boy in romping, climbing, swimming,
playing whoop and ball. Among some of the Tartar tribes of

the present day, women manage a horse, hurl a javelin, hunt wild animals, and fight an enemy as well as a man. The Indian women endure fatigues and carry burdens that some of our fair-faced, soft-handed, moustached young gentlemen would consider quite impossible for them to sustain. The Croatian and Wallachian women perform all the agricultural operations in addition to their domestic labors, and it is no uncommon sight in our cities, to see the German immigrant with his hands in his pockets, walking complacently by the side of his wife, whilst she bears the weight of some huge package or piece of furniture upon her head. Physically, as well as intellectually, it is use that produces growth and development.

But there is a class of objectors, who say they do not claim superiority, they merely assert a difference. But you will find by following them up closely, that they soon run this difference into the old groove of superiority. The phrenologist says that woman's head has just as many organs as man's, and that they are similarly situated. He says, too, that the organs most used are most prominent. They do not divide heads according to sex, but they call all the fine heads masculine, and the inferior feminine. When a woman presents a well-developed intellectual region, they say she has a masculine head, as if there could be nothing remarkable of the feminine gender. When a man has a small head, with little reasoning power, and the affections strongly developed, they say he has a woman's head, thus giving all reasoning power to the masculine gender.

Some say our heads are less,
Some men's are small, not they the least of men,
For often fineness compensates for size,
Besides the brain is like the hand, and grows with using.

The Civil and Political Rights of Women

We have met here to-day to discuss our rights and wrongs, civil and political, and not, as some have supposed, to go into the detail of social life alone. We do not propose to petition the legislature to make our husbands just, generous and courteous, to seat every man at the head of a cradle, and to clothe every woman in male attire. None of these points, however important they may be considered by leading men, will be touched in this Convention. As to their costume, the gentlemen need feel no fear of our imitating that, for we think it in violation of every principle of taste, beauty and dignity; notwithstanding all the contempt cast upon our loose, flowing garments, we still admire the graceful folds, and consider our costume far more artistic than theirs. Many of the nobler sex seem to agree with us in this opinion, for the bishops, priests, judges, barristers, and lordmayors of the first nation on the globe, and the Pope of Rome, with his Cardinals, too, all wear the loose flowing robes, thus tacitly acknowledging that the male attire is neither dignified nor imposing. No, we shall not molest you in your philosophical experiments with stocks, pants, high-heeled boots and Russian belts. Yours be the glory to discover, by personal experience, how long the knee-pan can resist the terrible strapping down which you impose, in how short time the well developed muscles of the throat can be reduced to mere threads by the constant pressure of the stock, how high the heel of a boot must be to make a short man tall, and how tight the Russian belt may be drawn and yet have wind enough left to sustain life. But we are assembled to protest against a form of government, existing without the consent of the governed—to declare our right to be free as man is free, to be represented in the government which we are taxed to support, to have such disgraceful laws as give man the power to chastise and imprison his wife, to take the wages which she earns, the property which she inherits, and, in case of separation, the children of her love; laws which make her the mere dependent on his bounty. It is to protest against such unjust laws as these that we are assembled to-day, and to have them, if possible, forever erased from our statute books, deeming them a shame and a disgrace to a Christian republic in the nineteenth century. We have met

> To uplift woman's fallen divinity
> Upon an even pedestal with man's.

And, strange as it may seem to many, we now demand our right to vote according to the declaration of the government under which we live. This right no one pretends to deny. We need not prove ourselves equal to Daniel Webster[9] to enjoy this privilege, for the ignorant Irishman in the ditch has all the civil rights he has. We need not prove our muscular power equal to this same Irishman to enjoy this privilege, for the most tiny, weak, ill-shaped stripling of twenty-one, has all the civil rights of the Irishman. We have no objection to discuss the question of equality, for we feel that the weight of argument lies wholly with us, but we wish the question of equality kept distinct from the question of rights, for the proof of the one does not determine the truth of the other. All white men in this country have the same rights, however they may differ in mind, body or estate. The right is ours. The question now is, how shall we get possession of what rightfully belongs to us. We should not feel so sorely grieved if no man who had not attained the full stature of a Webster, Clay, Van Buren, or Gerrit Smith could claim the right of the elective franchise.[10] But to have drunkards, idiots, horse-racing, rum-selling rowdies, ignorant foreigners and silly boys fully recognized, while we ourselves are thrust out from all the rights that belong to citizens, it is too grossly insulting to the dignity of woman to be longer quietly submitted to. The right is ours. Have it, we must. Use it, we will. The pens, the tongues, the fortunes, the indomitable wills of many women are already pledged to secure this right. The great truth, that no just government can be formed without the consent of the governed, we shall echo and re-echo in the ears of the unjust judge, until by continual coming we shall weary him.

But, say some, would you have woman vote? What, refined, delicate women at the polls, mingling in such scenes of violence and vulgarity? Most certainly. Where there is so much to be feared for the pure, the innocent, the noble, the mother surely should be there to watch and guard her sons who must encounter such stormy, dangerous scenes at the tender age of twenty-one. Much is said of woman's influence, might not her presence do much toward softening down this violence, refining this vulgarity? Depend upon it, the places that, by their impure atmosphere, are unfit for women, cannot but be dangerous to her sires and sons.

But, if woman claims all the rights of a citizen, will she buckle on her armor and fight in defense of her country? Has not woman already often shown herself as courageous in the field, as wise and patriotic in counsel as man? But for myself, I think all war sinful. I believe in Christ. I believe that command, "resist not evil" [Matt. 5:39], to be divine. "Vengeance is mine, and I will repay, saith the Lord" [Rom. 12:19]. Let frail man, who cannot foresee the consequences of an action, walk humbly with his God, loving his enemies, blessing them who curse him, and always returning good for evil. This is the highest kind of courage that mortal man can attain to. And this moral warfare with our own bad passions requires no physical power to achieve. I would not have man go to war. I can see no glory in fighting with such weapons as guns and swords, whilst man has in his possession the infinitely superior ones of righteousness and truth.

But what would woman gain by voting? Men must know the advantages of voting, for they all seem very tenacious about the right. Think you, if woman had a voice in this government, that all those laws affecting her interests would so entirely violate every principle of right and justice? Had woman a vote to give, might not the office-holders and seekers propose some change in her condition? Might not Woman's Rights become as great a question as free soil?

"But are you not already represented by your fathers, husbands, brothers and sons?" Let your statute books answer the question. We have had enough of such representation. In nothing is woman's true happiness consulted. Men like to call her an angel—to feed her on what they think sweet food—nourishing her vanity; to make her believe that her organization is so much finer than theirs, that she is not fitted to struggle with the tempests of public life, but needs their care and protection!! Care and protection—such as the wolf gives the lamb—such as the eagle the hare he carries to his eyrie!! Most cunningly he entraps her, and then takes from her all those rights which are dearer to him than life itself—rights which have been baptized in blood—and the maintenance of which is even now rocking to their foundations the kingdoms of the Old World. . . .

The voice of woman has been silenced in the state, the church, and the home, but man cannot fulfill his destiny alone, he cannot redeem his race unaided. There are deep and tender chords of sympathy and love in the hearts of the down-fallen and oppressed that woman can touch more skill-fully than man. The world has never yet seen a truly great and virtuous nation, because in the degradation of woman the very fountains of life are poisoned at their source. It is vain to look for silver and gold from mines of copper and lead. It is the wise mother that has the wise son. So long as your women are slaves you may throw your colleges and churches to the winds. You can't have scholars and saints so long as your mothers are ground to powder between the upper and nether millstone of tyranny and lust. How seldom, now, is a father's pride gratified, his fond hopes realized, in the budding genius of his son. The wife is degraded, made the mere creature of caprice, and the foolish son is heaviness to his heart. Truly are the sins of the fathers visited upon the children to the third and fourth generation. God, in His wisdom, has so linked the whole human family together, that any violence done at one end of the chain is felt throughout its length, and here, too, is the law of restoration, as in woman all have fallen, so in her elevation shall the race be recreated. "Voices" were the visitors and advisers of Joan of Arc. Do not "voices" come to us daily from the haunts of poverty, sorrow, degradation and despair, already too long unheeded. Now is the time for the women of this country, if they would save our free institutions, to defend the right, to buckle on the armor that can best resist the keenest weapons of the enemy—contempt and ridicule. The same religious enthusiasm that nerved Joan of Arc to her work nerves us to ours. In every generation God calls some men and women for the utterance of truth, a heroic action, and our work to-day is the fulfilling of what has long since been foretold by the Prophet—Joel 2:28: "And it shall come to pass afterward, that I will pour out my spirit upon all flesh, and your sons and your daughters shall prophesy." We do not expect our path will be strewn with the flowers of popular applause, but over the thorns of bigotry and prejudice will be our way, and on our banners will beat the dark storm-clouds of opposition from those who have entrenched themselves behind the stormy bulwarks of custom and authority, and who have fortified their position by every means, holy and unholy. But we will steadfastly abide the result. Unmoved we will bear it

Discourse on Woman

Lucretia Mott

Lucretia Mott's views on women's rights were shaped by
her upbringing as a Quaker, a religion that regards men
and women as equals. Her fiery oratorical skills earned
her a position as a Quaker minister and attracted wide
audiences to the women's rights conventions where she
lectured. Mott, like many others involved in the women's
movement, was also a passionate abolitionist.

The following speech, delivered to a Philadelphia audience in 1849, is Mott's response to a popular lecture on
womanhood by poet and essayist Richard Henry Dana,
in which he "ridiculed [women's] demands for civil and
political rights, and for a larger sphere of action." Here,
Mott draws on her knowledge of biblical texts to rebut
claims that the Bible justifies society's unequal treatment
of women.

There is nothing of greater importance to the well-being
of society at large—of man as well as woman—than
the true and proper position of woman. Much has
been said, from time to time, upon this subject. It has been a
theme for ridicule, for satire and sarcasm. We might look for
this from the ignorant and vulgar; but from the intelligent
and refined we have a right to expect that such weapons shall
not be resorted to—that gross comparisons and vulgar epi-
thets shall not be applied, so as to place woman, in a point
of view, ridiculous to say the least.

From Lucretia Mott, "Discourse on Woman," speech delivered in Philadelphia,
Pennsylvania, December 17, 1849.

This subject has claimed my earnest interest for many years. I have long wished to see woman occupying a more elevated position than that which custom for ages has allotted to her. It was with great regret, therefore, that I listened a few days ago to a lecture upon this subject, which, though replete with intellectual beauty, and containing much that was true and excellent, was yet fraught with sentiments calculated to retard the progress of woman to the high elevation destined by her Creator. I regretted the more that these sentiments should be presented with such intellectual vigor and beauty, because they would be likely to ensnare the young. . . .

Men and Women Were Created Equal

In the beginning, man and woman were created equal. "Male and female created he them, and blessed them, and called their name Adam" [Gen. 1:27]. He gave dominion to both over the lower animals, but not to one over the other.

> Man o'er woman
> He made not lord, such title to himself
> Reserving, human left from human free."[1]

The cause of the subjection of woman to man, was early ascribed to disobedience to the command of God. This would seem to show that she was then regarded as not occupying her true and rightful position in society.[2]

The laws given on Mount Sinai for the government of man and woman were equal, the precepts of Jesus make no distinction. Those who read the Scriptures, and judge for themselves, not resting satisfied with the perverted application of the text, do not find the distinction, that theology and ecclesiastical authorities have made, in the condition of the sexes. In the early ages, Miriam [Exod. 15:20] and Deborah [Judg. 4, 5], conjointly with Aaron and Barak, enlisted themselves on the side which they regarded the right, unitedly going up to their battles, and singing their songs of victory. We regard these with veneration. Deborah judged Israel many years—she went up with Barak against their enemies, with an army of 10,000, assuring him that the honor of the battle should not be to him, but to a woman. Revolting as were the circumstances of their success, the acts of a semi-barbarous people, yet we read with reverence the song of Deborah:

> Blessed above woman shall Jael, the wife of Heeber, the Kenite be; blessed shall she be above women in the tent. . . . She put her hand to the nail, and her right hand to the workman's hammer; she smote Sisera through his temples. At her feet he bowed, he fell, he lay down dead [Judg. 5:24, 26–27].

This circumstance, revolting to Christianity, is recognized as an act befitting woman in that day. Deborah, Huldah [2 Kings 22:14], and other honorable women, were looked up to and consulted in times of exigency, and their counsel was received. In that eastern country, with all the customs tending to degrade woman, some were called to fill great and important stations in society. There were also false prophetesses as well as true. The denunciations of Ezekiel were upon those women who would "prophesy out of their own heart, and sew pillows to all armholes" [14:17], &c.

Coming down to later times, we find Anna [Luke 2:36], a prophetess of four-score years, in the temple day and night, speaking of Christ to all them who looked for redemption in Jerusalem. Numbers of women were the companions of Jesus [Matt. 26:55]—one going to the men of the city, saying, "Come, see a man who told me all things that ever I did; is not this the Christ?" [John 4:29]. Another, "Whatsoever he saith unto you, do it" [John 2:5]. Philip had four daughters who did prophesy [Acts 21:8]. Tryphena and Tryphosa [Rom. 16:12] were co-workers with the apostles in their mission, to whom they sent special messages of regard and acknowledgement of their labors in the gospel. A learned Jew, mighty in the Scriptures, was by Priscilla instructed in the way of the Lord more perfectly [Acts 18:2]. Phebe [Rom. 16:1] is mentioned as a *servant* of Christ, and commended as such to the brethren. It is worthy of note, that the word *servant*, when applied to Tychicus [Eph. 6:21: Col. 4:7], is rendered *minister*. Women *professing* godliness, should be translated *preaching*.

The first announcement, on the day of Pentecost, was the fulfillment of ancient prophecy, that God's spirit should be poured out upon *daughters* as well as sons, and they should prophesy [Joel 2:28; Acts 2:17]. It is important that we be familiar with these facts, because woman has been so long circumscribed in her influence by the perverted application of the text, rendering it improper for her to speak in the assemblies of the people, "to edification, to exhortation, and to comfort" [1 Cor. 14:3].

Lucretia Mott

If these scriptures were read intelligently, we should not so learn Christ, as to exclude any from a position, where they might exert an influence for good to their fellow-beings. The epistle to the Corinthian church, where the supposed apostolic prohibition of women's preaching is found, contains express directions how woman shall appear, when she prayeth or prophesyeth [1 Cor. 14]. Judge then whether this admonition, relative to *speaking* and asking questions, in the excited state of that church, should be regarded as a standing injunction on woman's *preaching*, when that word was not used by the apostle. Where is the Scripture authority for the advice given to the early church, under peculiar circumstances, being binding on the church of the present day? Ecclesiastical history informs us, that for two or three hundred years, female ministers suffered martyrdom, in the company with their brethren.

These things are too much lost sight of. They should be known, in order that we may be prepared to meet the assertion, so often made, that woman is stepping out of her appropriate sphere, when she shall attempt to instruct public assemblies. The present time particularly demands such investigation. It requires also, that "of yourselves ye should judge what is right" [Luke 12:57] that you should know the ground whereon you stand. This age is notable for its works of mercy and benevolence—for the efforts that are made to reform the inebriate and the degraded, to relieve the oppressed and the suffering. Women as well as men are interested in these works of justice and mercy. They are efficient co-workers, their talents are called into profitable exercise, their labors are effective in each department of reform. The blessing to the merciful, to the peacemaker [Matt. 5:7, 9] is equal to man and to woman. It is greatly to be deplored, now that she is increasingly qualified for usefulness, that any view should be presented, calculated to retard her labors of love.

Woman as a Reformer

Why should not woman seek to be a reformer? If she is to shrink from being such an iconoclast as shall "break the image of man's lower worship," as so long held up to view; if she is to fear to exercise her reason, and her noblest powers, lest she should be thought to "attempt to act the man," and not "acknowledge his supremacy"; if she is to be satisfied with the narrow sphere assigned her by man, nor aspire to a higher, lest she should transcend the bounds of female delicacy; truly it is a mournful prospect for woman. We would admit all the difference, that our great and beneficent Creator has made, in the relation of man and woman, nor would we seek to disturb this relation; but we deny that the present position of woman, is her true sphere of usefulness; nor will she attain to this sphere, until the disabilities and disadvantages, religious, civil, and social, which impede her progress, are removed out of her way. These restrictions have enervated her mind and paralysed her powers. While man assumes, that the present is the original state designed for woman, that the *existing* "differences are not arbitrary nor the result of accident," but grounded in nature; she will not make the necessary effort to obtain her just rights, lest it should subject her to the kind of scorn and contemptuous manner in which she has been spoken of. . . .

What Women Are Seeking

The question is often asked, "What does woman want, more than she enjoys?" What is she seeking to obtain? Of what rights is she deprived? What privileges are withheld from her? I answer, she asks nothing as favor, but as right, she wants to be acknowledged a moral, responsible being. She is seeking not to be governed by laws, in the making of which she has no voice. She is deprived of almost every right in civil society, and is a cypher in the nation, except in the right of presenting a petition. In religious society her disabilities, as already pointed out, have greatly retarded her progress. Her exclusion from the pulpit or ministry—her duties marked out for her by her equal brother man, subject to creeds, rules, and disciplines made for her by him—this is unworthy her true dignity. In marriage, there is assumed superiority, on the part of the husband, and admitted inferiority, with a promise of obedience, on the part of the wife. This subject calls loudly for examination, in order that the wrong may be redressed. Customs suited to darker ages in Eastern countries, are not binding upon enlightened society. The solemn covenant of marriage may be entered into without these lordly assumptions, and humiliating concessions and promises.

There are large Christian denominations who [sic] do not recognize such degrading relations of husband and wife. They ask no magisterial or ministerial aid to legalize or to sanctify this union. But acknowledging themselves in the presence of the Highest, and invoking his assistance, they come under reciprocal obligations of fidelity and affection, before suitable witnesses. Experience and observation go to prove, that there may be as much harmony, to say the least, in such a union, and as great purity and permanency of affection, as can exist where the more common custom or form is observed. The distinctive relations of husband and wife, of father and mother of a family are sacredly preserved, without the assumption of authority on the one part, or the promise of obedience on the other. There is nothing in such a marriage degrading to woman. She does not compromise her dignity or self-respect; but enters married life upon equal ground, by the side of her husband. By proper education, she understands her duties, physical, intellectual and moral; and fulfilling these, she is a help meet, in the true sense of the word.

I tread upon delicate ground in alluding to the institutions of religious associations; but the subject is of so much importance, that all which relates to the position of woman, should be examined, apart from the undue veneration which ancient usage receives.

Such dupes are men to custom, and so prone
To reverence what is ancient, and can plead
A course of long observance for its use,
That even servitude, the worst of ills,
Because delivered down from sire to son,
Is kept and guarded as a sacred thing.

So with woman. She has so long been subject to the disabilities and restrictions, with which her progress has been
embarrassed, that she has become enervated, her mind to
some extent paralysed; and, like those still more degraded by
personal bondage, she hugs her chains. Liberty is often presented in its true light, but it is liberty for man.

Whose freedom is by suffrance, and at will
Of a superior—he is never free.
Who lives, and is not weary of a life
Exposed to manacles, deserves them well.[3]

I would not, however, go so far, either as regards the abject slave or woman; for in both cases they may be so degraded by the crushing influences around them, that they
may not be sensible of the blessing of Freedom. Liberty is not
less a blessing, because oppression has so long darkened the
mind that it cannot appreciate it. I would therefore urge, that
woman be placed in such a situation in society, by the yield-
ing of her rights, and have such opportunities for growth and
development, as shall raise her from this low, enervated and
paralysed condition, to a full appreciation of the blessing of
entire freedom of mind.

A Case for the Political Rights of Women

It is with reluctance that I make the demand for the political
rights of woman, because this claim is so distasteful to the
age. Woman shrinks, in the present state of society, from taking any interest in politics. The events of the French Revolution, and the claim for woman's rights are held up to her as
a warning. But let us not look at the excesses of women
alone, at that period; but remember that the age was marked
with extravagances and wickedness in men as well as
women. Indeed, political life abounds with these excesses,

and with shameful outrage. Who knows, but that if woman acted her part in governmental affairs, there might be an entire change in the turmoil of political life. It becomes man to speak modestly of his ability to act without her. If woman's judgment were exercised, why might she not aid in making the laws by which she is governed? Lord Brougham remarked that the works of Harriet Martineau upon Political Economy were not excelled by those of any political writer of the present time. The first few chapters of her *Society in America* [1837], her views of a Republic, and of Government generally, furnish evidence of woman's capacity to embrace subjects of universal interest.

Far be it from me to encourage woman to vote, or to take an active part in politics, in the present state of our government. Her right to the elective franchise however, is the same, and should be yielded to her, whether she exercise that right or not. Would that man too, would have no participation in a government based upon the life-taking principle—upon retaliation and the sword. It is unworthy a Christian nation. But when, in the diffusion of light and intelligence, a convention shall be called to make regulations for self-government on Christian, non-resistant principles, I can see no good reason, why woman should not participate in such an assemblage, taking part equally with man.

Walker, of Cincinnati, in his *Introduction to American Law* [1837], says:

> With regard to political rights, females form a positive exception to the general doctrine of equality. They have no part or lot in the formation or administration of government. They cannot vote or hold office. We require them to contribute their share in the ways of taxes, to the support of government, but allow them no voice in its direction. We hold them amenable to the laws when made, but allow them no share in making them. This language, applied to males, would be the exact definition of political slavery; applied to females, custom does not teach us so to regard it.

Woman, however, is beginning so to regard it.

The law of husband and wife, as you gather it from the

books, is a disgrace to any civilized nation. The theory of the law degrades the wife almost to the level of slaves. When a woman marries, we call her condition coverture, and speak of her as a *femme covert*. The old writers call the husband baron, and sometimes, in plain English, lord. . . . The merging of her name in that of her husband is emblematic of the fate of all her legal rights. The torch of Hymen serves but to light the pile, on which these rights are offered up. The legal theory is, that marriage makes the husband and wife one person, and that person is the *husband*. On this subject, reform is loudly called for. There is no foundation in reason or expediency, for the absolute and slavish subjection of the wife to the husband, which forms the foundation of the present legal relations. Were woman, in point of fact, the abject thing which the law, in theory, considers her to be when married, she would not be worthy the companionship of man.[4]

I would ask if such a code of laws does not require change? If such a condition of the wife in society does not claim redress? On no good ground can reform be delayed. . . .

Let woman then go on—not asking as favor, but claiming as right, the removal of all the hindrances to her elevation in the scale of being—let her receive encouragement for the proper cultivation of all her powers, so that she may enter profitably into the active business of life; employing her own hands, in ministering to her necessities, strengthening her physical being by proper exercise, and observance of the laws of health. Let her not be ambitious to display a fair hand, and to promenade the fashionable streets of our city, but rather, coveting earnestly the best gifts, let her strive to occupy such walks in society, as will befit her true dignity in all the relations of life. No fear that she will then transcend the proper limits of female delicacy. True modesty will be as fully preserved, in acting out those important vocations to which she may be called, as in the nursery or at the fireside, ministering to man's self-indulgence.

Then in the marriage union, the independence of the husband and wife will be equal, their dependence mutual, and their obligations reciprocal.

In conclusion, let me say, "Credit not the old fashioned absurdity, that woman's is a secondary lot, ministering to the necessities of her lord and master! It is a higher destiny I would award you. If your immortality is as complete, and your gift of mind as capable as ours, of increase and elevation, I would put no wisdom of mine against God's evident allotment. I would charge you to water the undying bud, and give it healthy culture, and open its beauty to the sun—and then you may hope, that when your life is bound up with another, you will go on equally, and in a fellowship that shall pervade every earthly interest."[5]

Notes

1. Mott misquotes poet John Milton's *Paradise Lost*, 12.69–71: "But man over men/ He made not lord; such title to himself/ Reserving, human left from human free."

2. The Quaker religion, to which Mott subscribed, believed that Christ restored men and women to their original relationship of equality.

3. The poetry quoted in this section is from William Cowper, "The Task."

4. Timothy Walker (1802–1856), jurist and author.

5. The author of this quote is Nathaniel Parker Willis (1806–1867), author, playwright, and journalist.

After having heard the letter read from our poor incarcerated sisters of France, well might we exclaim, Alas! poor France! where is thy glory? Where the glory of the Revolution of 1848, in which shone forth the pure and magnanimous spirit of an oppressed nation, struggling for Freedom?[1] Where the fruits of that victory that gave to the world the motto, Liberty, Equality, and Fraternity? A motto destined to hurl the tyranny of kings and priests into the dust, and give freedom to the enslaved millions of the earth. Where, I again ask, is the result of these noble achievements, when Woman, ay, one half of the nation, is deprived of her rights? Has Woman then been idle during the contest between Right and Might? Has she been wanting in ardor and enthusiasm? Has she not mingled her blood with that of her husband, son, and sire? Or has she been recreant in hailing the motto of Liberty floating on your banners as an omen of justice, peace, and freedom to man, that at the first step she takes practically to claim the recognition of her Rights, she is rewarded with the doom of a martyr? But Right has not yet asserted her prerogative, for Might rules the day; and as every good cause must have its martyrs, why should Woman not be a martyr for her cause? But need we wonder that France, governed as she is by Russian and Austrian despotism, does not recognize the rights of humanity in the recognition of the Rights of Woman, when even here, in this far-famed land of freedom, under a Republic that has inscribed on its banner the great truth that all men are created free and equal, and endowed with inalienable rights to life, liberty, and the pursuit of happiness,—a declaration borne, like the vision of hope, on wings of light to the remotest parts of the earth, an omen of freedom to the oppressed and downtrodden children of man,—when, even here, in the very face of this eternal truth, woman, the mockingly so called "better half" of man, has yet to plead for her rights, nay, for her life; for what is life without liberty, and what is liberty without equality of rights? And as for the pursuit of happiness, she is not allowed to pursue any line of life that might promote it; she has only thankfully to accept what man in his magnanimity decides is best for her to do, and this is what he does not choose to do himself. Is she then not included in that declaration? Answer, ye wise men of the nation, and answer truly; add not hypocrisy to oppression! Say that she is not created free and equal, and therefore (for the sequence follows on the premises) that she is not entitled to life, liberty, and the pursuit of happiness. But with all the audacity arising from an assumed superiority, you dare not so libel and insult humanity as to say, that she is not included in that declaration; and if she is, then what right has man, except that of might, to deprive woman of the rights and privileges he claims for himself? And why, in the name of reason and justice, why should she not have the same rights? Because she is woman? Humanity recognizes no sex—virtue recognizes no sex—mind recognizes no sex—life and death, pleasure and pain, happiness and misery recognize no sex. Like man, woman comes involuntarily into existence; like him she possesses physical and mental and moral powers, on the proper cultivation of which depends her happiness; like him she is subject to all the vicissitudes of life; like him she has to pay the penalty for disobeying nature's laws, and far greater penalties has she to suffer from ignorance of her far more complicated nature than he; like him she enjoys or suffers with her country. Yet she is not recognized as his equal! In the laws of the land she has no rights, in government she has no voice. And in spite of another principle, recognized in this Republic, namely, that "taxation without representation is tyranny," yet she is taxed without being represented. Her property may be consumed by taxes to defray the expenses of that unholy, unrighteous custom called war, yet she has no power to give her veto against it. From the cradle to the grave she is subject to the power and control of man. Father, guardian, or husband, one conveys her like some piece of merchandise over to the other. At marriage she loses her entire identity and her being is said to have become merged in her husband. Has nature thus merged it? Has she ceased to exist and feel pleasure and pain? When she violates the laws of her being, does her husband pay the penalty? When she breaks the moral laws, does he suffer the punishment? When he supplies his wants, is it enough to satisfy her nature? And when at his nightly orgies, in the grog-shop and the oyster cellar, or at the gaming-table, he squanders the means she helped by her cooperation and economy to accumulate, and she awakens to penury and destitution, will it supply the wants of her children to tell them, that owing to the superiority of man she had no redress by law; and that as her being was merged in his, so also ought theirs to be? What an inconsistency, that from the moment she enters that compact, in which she assumes the high responsibility of wife and mother, she ceases legally to exist, and becomes a purely submissive being. Blind submission in woman is considered a virtue, while submission to wrong is itself wrong, and resistance to wrong is virtue alike in woman as in man.

The Husband Keeps His Wife

But it will be said that the husband provides for the wife, or in other words, he feeds, clothes, and shelters her! I wish I had the power to make every one before me fully realize the degradation contained in that idea. Yes! he *keeps* her, and so he does a favorite horse; by law they are both considered his property. Both may, when the cruelty of the owner compels them to run away, be brought back by the strong arm of the law, and according to a still extant law of England both may be led by the halter to the marketplace and sold. This is humiliating indeed, but nevertheless true; and the sooner these things are known and understood, the better for humanity. It is no fancy sketch. I know that some endeavor to throw the mantle of romance over the subject, and treat woman like some ideal existence, not liable to the ills of life. Let such deal in fancy, that have nothing better to deal in; we have to do with sober, sad realities, with stubborn facts.

Again, I shall be told that the law presumes the husband to be kind, affectionate, and ready to provide for and protect his wife. But what right, I ask, has the law to presume at all on the subject? What right has the law to intrust the interest and happiness of one being into the hands of another? And if the merging of the interest of one being into the other is a necessary consequence on marriage, why should woman always remain on the losing side? Turn the tables. Let the identity and interest of the husband be merged in the wife. Think you she would act less generously towards him, than he towards her?

Think you she is not capable of as much justice, disinterested devotion, and abiding affection, as he is? Oh, how grossly you misunderstand and wrong her nature! But we desire no such undue power over man; it would be as wrong in her to exercise it as it now is in him. All we claim is an equal legal and social position. We have nothing to do with individual man, be he good or bad, but with the laws that oppress woman. We know that bad and unjust laws must in the nature of things make man so too. If he is kind, affectionate, and consistent, it is because the kindlier feelings, instilled by a mother, kept warm by a sister, and cherished by a wife, will not allow him to carry out those barbarous laws against woman.

But the estimation she is generally held in, is as degrading as it is foolish. Man forgets that woman cannot be degraded without its re-acting on himself. The impress of her mind is stamped on him by nature, and the early education of the mother which no after-training can entirely efface; and therefore, the estimation she is held in falls back with double force upon him. Yet, from the force of prejudice against her, he knows it not. Not long ago, I saw an account of two offenders, brought before a Justice of New York. One was charged with stealing a pair of boots, for which offense he was sentenced to six months' imprisonment; the other crime was assault and battery upon his wife: he was let off with a reprimand from the judge! With my principles, I am entirely opposed to punishment, and hold, that to reform the erring and remove the causes of evil is much more efficient, as well as just, than to punish. But the judge showed us the comparative value which he set on these two kinds of *property*. But then you must remember that the boots were taken by a stranger, while the wife was insulted by her legal owner! Here it will be said, that such degrading cases are but few. For the sake of humanity, I hope they are. But as long as woman shall be oppressed by unequal laws, so long will she be degraded by man. . . .

The Principle of Universal Suffrage

Carry out the republican principle of universal suffrage, or strike it from your banners and substitute "Freedom and

Power to one half of society, and submission and slavery to the other." Give woman the elective franchise. Let married women have the same right to property that their husbands have; for whatever the difference in their respective occupations, the duties of the wife are as indispensable and far more arduous than the husband's. Why then should the wife, at the death of her husband, not be his heir to the same extent that he is heir to her? In this inequality there is involved another wrong. When the wife dies, the husband is left in the undisturbed possession of all there is, and the children are left with him; no change is made, no stranger intrudes on his home and his affliction. But when the husband dies, not only is the widow, as too often is the case, deprived of all, and at best receives but a mere pittance, while strangers assume authority denied to the wife. The sanctuary of affliction must be desecrated by executors; everything must be ransacked and assessed, lest she should steal something out of her own house; and to cap the climax, the children must be placed under guardians. When the husband dies poor, to be sure, no guardian is required, and the children are left for the mother to care and toil for them, as best she may. But when anything is left for their maintenance, then it must be placed in the hands of strangers for safe keeping! The bringing up and safety of the children is left with the mother, and safe they are in her hands. But a few hundred or thousand dollars cannot be intrusted with her! But, say they, "in case of a second marriage, the children must be protected in their possession." Does that reason not hold as good in the case of the husband as in that of the wife? Oh, no! When *he* marries again, he still retains his identity and power to act; but *she* becomes merged once more into a mere nonentity; and therefore the first husband must rob her to prevent the second from doing so! Make the laws then, (if any are required,) regulating property between husband and wife, equal for both, and all these difficulties would be removed.

According to a late act, the wife has a right to the property she brings at marriage, or receives in any way after marriage.[2] Here is some provision for the favored few; but for the laboring many, there is none. The mass of the people commence life with no other capital than the union of heads, hearts and hands. To the benefit of this best of capital, the wife has no right. If they are unsuccessful in married life, who suffers more the bitter consequences of poverty than the wife? But if successful, she cannot call a dollar her own. The husband may will away every dollar of the personal property, and leave her destitute and penniless, and she has no redress by law. And even where real estate is left, she receives but a life-interest in a third part of it, and at her death, she cannot leave it to any one belonging to her, it falls back even to the remotest of his relatives. This is law, but where is the justice of it? Well might we say that laws were made to prevent, not to promote, the ends of justice. Or, in case of separation, why should the children be taken from the protecting care of the mother? Who has a better right to them than she? . . .

It is high time to denounce such gross injustice, to compel man by the might of right to give to woman her political, legal, and social rights. Open to her all the avenues of emolument, distinction, and greatness; give her an object for which to cultivate her powers, and a fair chance to do so, and there will be no need to speculate as to her proper sphere. She will find her own sphere in accordance with her capacities, powers, and tastes; and yet she will be woman still. Her rights will not change, but strengthen, develop, and elevate her nature. Away, then, with that folly and absurdity, that a possession of her rights would be detrimental to her character; that if she is recognized as the equal to man, she would cease to be woman. Have his rights as citizen of a republic, the elective franchise with all its advantages, so changed man's nature, that he has ceased to be man? Oh, no! But woman could not bear such a degree of power; what has benefited him, would injure her; what has strengthened him, would weaken her; what has prompted him to the performance of his duties, would make her neglect hers! Such is the superficial mode of reasoning—if it deserves that name— which is brought against the doctrine of woman's equality with man. It reminds me of two reasons given by a minister of Milton, on the North River. Having heard that I had spoken on the Rights of Woman, he took the subject up on the following Sunday; and in order to prove that woman should not have equal rights with man, he argued, first, that Adam was created before Eve, and secondly, that man was compared to the fore wheels, and woman to the hind wheels of a wagon. These reasons are about as philosophical as any that can be brought against the views we advocate.

But here is another difficulty. In point of principle, some say it is true that woman ought to have the same rights as man; but in carrying out this principle in practice, would you expose her to the contact of rough, rude, drinking, swearing, fighting men at the ballot-box? What a humiliating confession lies in this plea for keeping woman in the background! Is the brutality of some men, then, a reason why woman should be kept from her rights? If man, in his superior wisdom, cannot devise means to enable woman to deposit her vote without having her finer sensibilities shocked by such disgraceful conduct, then there is an additional reason, as well as necessity, why she should be there to civilize, refine, and purify him, even at the ballot-box. . . .

Oh! blind and misguided man! you know not what you do in opposing this great reform. It is not a partial affair confined to class, sect, or party. Nations have ever struggled against nations, people against despotic governments; from the times of absolute despotism to the present hour of comparative freedom, the weak have had to struggle against the strong, and right against might. But a new sign has appeared in our social zodiac, prophetic of the most important changes, pregnant with the most beneficial results, that have ever taken place in the annals of human history. We have before us a novel spectacle, an hitherto unheard-of undertaking, in comparison to which all others fall into insignificance, the grandest step in the onward progress of humanity. *One half of the race* stands up against the injustice and oppression of the other, and demands the recognition of its existence, and of its rights. Most sincerely do I pity those who have not advanced far enough to aid in this noble undertaking; for the attainment of woman's coequality with man is in itself not the *end,* but the most efficient *means* ever at the command of mankind towards a higher state of human elevation, without which the race can never attain it. Why should one half of the race keep the other half in subjugation? In this country it is considered wrong for one nation to enact laws and force them upon another. Does the same wrong not hold good of the sexes? Is woman a being like man? Then she is entitled to the same rights, is she not? How can he legislate rightfully for a being whose nature he cannot understand, whose motives he cannot appreciate, and whose feelings he cannot realize? How can he sit in judgment and pronounce a verdict against a being so entirely different from himself?

Falsehoods Propagated Against Women

No! there is no reason against woman's elevation, but there are deep-rooted, hoary-headed prejudices. The main cause of them is, a pernicious falsehood propagated against her being, namely, that she is inferior by her nature. Inferior in what? What has man ever done, that woman, under the same advantages, could not do? In morals, bad as she is, she is generally considered his superior. In the intellectual sphere, give her a fair chance before you pronounce a verdict against her. Cultivate the frontal portion of her brain as much as that of man is cultivated, and she will stand his equal at least. Even now, where her mind has been called out at all, her intellect is as bright, as capacious, and as powerful as his. Will you tell us, that women have no Newtons, Shakespeares, and Byrons? Greater natural powers than even these possessed may have been destroyed in woman for want of proper culture, a just appreciation, reward for merit as an incentive to exertion, and freedom of action, without which, mind becomes cramped and stifled, for it cannot expand under bolts and bars; and yet, amid all blighting, crushing circumstances— confined within the narrowest possible limits, trampled upon by prejudice and injustice, from her education and position forced to occupy herself almost exclusively with the most trivial affairs—in spite of all these difficulties, her intellect is as good as his. The few bright meteors in man's intellectual horizon could well be matched by woman, were she allowed to occupy the same elevated position. There is no need of naming the De Staëls,[3] the Rolands,[4] the Somervilles,[5] the Wollstonecrafts,[6] the Sigourneys,[7] the Wrights,[8] the Martineaus,[9] the Hemanses,[10] the Fullers,[11] Jagellos [sic],[12] and many more of modern as well as ancient times, to prove her mental powers, her patriotism, her self-sacrificing devotion to the cause of humanity, and the eloquence that gushes from her pen, or from her tongue. These things are too well known to require repetition. And do you ask for fortitude, energy, and perseverance? Then look at woman under suffering, reverse of fortune, and affliction, when the strength and power of man have sunk to the lowest ebb, when his mind is overwhelmed by the dark waters of despair. She, like the tender ivy plant, bent yet unbroken by the storms of life, not only upholds her own hopeful courage, but clings around the tempest-fallen oak, to speak hope to his faltering spirit, and shelter him from the returning blast of the storm.

Wherein then, again I ask, is man so much woman's superior, that he must for ever remain her master? In physical strength? Allow me to say, that therein the inmates of the forest are his superior. But even on this point, why is she the feeble, sickly, suffering being we behold her? Look to her most defective and irrational education, and you will find a solution of the problem. Is the girl allowed to expand her limbs and chest in healthful exercise in the fresh breezes of heaven? Is she allowed to inflate her lungs and make the welkin ring with her cheerful voice like the boy? Who ever heard of a girl committing such improprieties? A robust development in a girl is unfashionable, a healthy, sound voice is vulgar, a ruddy glow on the cheek is coarse; and when vitality is so strong within her as to show itself in spite of bolts and bars, then she has to undergo a bleaching process, eat lemons, drink vinegar, and keep in the shade.

And do you know why these irrationalities are practised? Because man wishes them to be delicate; for whatever he admires in woman will she possess. That is the influence man has over woman, for she has been made to believe that she was created for his benefit only. "It was not well for man to be alone" [Gen. 2:18], therefore she was made as a plaything to pass away an idle hour, or as a drudge to do his bidding; and until this falsehood is eradicated from her mind, until she feels that the necessities, services, and obligations of the sexes are mutual, that she is as independent of him as he is of her, that she is formed for the same aims and ends in life that he is—until, in fact, she has all rights equal with man, there will be no other object in her education, except to get married, and what will best promote that desirable end will be cultivated in her. Do you not yet understand what has made woman what she is? Then see what the sickly taste and perverted judgment of man now admires in woman. Not physical and mental vigor, but a pale, delicate face; hands too small to grasp a broom, for that were treason in a lady; a voice so sentimental and depressed, that what she says can be learned only by the moving of her half parted lips; and above all, that nervous sensibility which sees a ghost in every passing shadow, that beautiful diffidence which dares not take a step without the protecting arm of man to support her tender frame, and that shrinking mock-modesty that faints at the mention of a leg of a table. I know there are many noble exceptions, who see and deplore these irrationalities; but as a general thing, the facts are as I state, or else why that hue and cry of "mannish," "unfeminine," "out of her sphere," etc., whenever woman evinces any strength of body or mind, and takes interest in anything deserving of a rational being? Oh! the crying injustice towards woman. She is crushed at every step, and then insulted for being what a most pernicious education and corrupt public sentiment have made her. But there is no confidence in her powers, nor principles. . . .

Man's Ignorance

It is from ignorance, not malice, that man acts towards woman as he does. In ignorance of her nature, and the interest and happiness of both sexes, he conceived ideas, laid down rules, and enacted laws concerning her destiny and rights. The same ignorance, strengthened by age, sanctified by superstition, ingrafted into his being by habit, makes him carry these convictions out to the detriment of his own as well as her happiness; for is he not the loser by his injustice? Oh! how severely he suffers. Who can fathom the depth of misery and suffering to society from the subjugation and injury inflicted on woman? The race is elevated in excellence and power, or kept back in progression, in accordance with the scale of woman's position in society. But so firmly has prejudice closed the eyes of man to the light of truth, that though he feels the evils, he knows not their cause. Those men who have their eyes already open to these facts, earnestly desire the restoration of woman's rights, as the means of enabling her to take her proper position in the scale of humanity. If all men could see the truth, all would desire to aid this reform, as they desire their own happiness; for the interest and happiness of the sexes cannot be divided. Nature has too closely united them to permit one to oppress the other with impunity. I cast no more blame or reproach on man, however, than on woman, for she, from habit based on the same errors, is as much opposed to her interest and happiness as he is. How long is it, indeed, since any of us have come out of the darkness into the light of day? How long since any of us have advocated this righteous cause? The longest period is but, as it were, yesterday. And why has this been? From the same reason that so many of both sexes are opposed to it yet—ignorance. Both men and women have to be roused from that deathly lethargy in which they slumber. That worse than Egyptian darkness must be dispelled from their minds before the pure rays of the sun can penetrate them. And therefore, while I feel it my duty, ay, a painful duty, to point out the wrong done to woman and its consequences, and would do all in my power to aid in her deliverance, I can have no more ill feelings towards man than, for the same error, I have towards her. Both are the victims of error and ignorance, both suffer. Hence the necessity for active, earnest endeavors to enlighten their minds; hence the necessity for this, and many more Conventions, to protest against the wrong and claim our rights. And in so acting, we must not heed the taunts, ridicule, and stigmas cast upon us. We must remember that we have a crusade before us, far holier and more righteous than led warriors to Palestine—a crusade, not to deprive any one of his rights, but to claim our own. And as our cause is a nobler one, so also should be the means to achieve it. We therefore must put on the armor of charity, carry before us the banner of truth, and defend ourselves with the shield of right against the invaders of our liberty. And yet, like the knight of old, we must enlist in this holy cause with a disinterested devotion, energy, and determination never to turn back until we have conquered, not, indeed, by driving the Turk from his possession, but by claiming our rightful inheritance, for his benefit as well as for our own. To achieve this glorious victory of right over might, woman has much to do. Man may remove her legal shackles, and recognize her as his equal, which will greatly aid in her elevation; but the law cannot compel her to cultivate her mind and take an independent stand as a free being. She must cast off that mountain weight, that intimidating cowardly question, which like a nightmare presses down all her energies, namely, "What will people say? what will Mrs. Grundy say?" Away with such slavish fears! Woman must think for herself, and use for herself that greatest of all prerogatives— judgment of right and wrong. And next she must act according to her best convictions, irrespective of any other voice than that of right and duty. The time, I trust, will come, though slowly, yet surely, when woman will occupy that high and lofty position, for which nature has so eminently fitted her, in the destinies of humanity.

Notes

1. In July 1851, French women's final attempt to gain suffrage failed.

2. The Married Woman's Property Act of 1848.

3. Feminist author Anne Louise Germaine Necker De Staël (1766–1817).

4. Jeanne Manon Philipon Roland de la Platière (1754–1793), French revolutionary.

5. Mary Somerville (1780–1872), Scottish mathematician and author of scientific works.

6. Mary Wollstonecraft (1759–1797), British author of the feminist treatise *A Vindication of the Rights of Woman*, published in 1792.

7. Author Lydia Howard Huntley Sigourney (1791–1865).

8. Frances Wright (1795–1852), a Scottish freethinker and socialist who advocated universal education, women's equality, religious freedom, and the abolition of slavery. It is said that she was the first woman in the United States to speak in public to audiences of men and women.

9. Harriet Martineau (1802–1876), English author on religion, economics, and government.

10. English poet Felicia Browne Hemans (1793–1835).

11. Margaret Fuller (1810–1850), author, critic, teacher, and feminist who led philosophical discussion groups in New England.

12. Appolonia Jagiello (1825–1866) fought for the liberation of Poland and Hungary.

Aren't I a Woman?

Sojourner Truth

After she left slavery in 1826, one year before her legal emancipation by New York State, Isabella Baumfree became a born-again Christian and changed her name to Sojourner Truth, which means "itinerant preacher." She traveled the east coast preaching the word of Christ and speaking on such subjects as abolition, the rights of freed slaves, and the rights of women. Unlike most other prominent activists of the time, Truth was illiterate and had no formal education; however, her commanding presence and artful manner of speaking awed crowds.

The first speech that follows was delivered to the woman's rights convention in Akron, Ohio, in 1851. It was recorded in writing by Frances D. Gage, who presided at the convention and insisted that Truth be allowed to speak despite objections from members of the audience. Gage describes the effect Truth had on her listeners:

> I rose and announced "Sojourner Truth," and begged the audience to keep silence for a few moments. The tumult subsided at once, and every eye was fixed on this almost Amazon form, which stood nearly six feet high, head erect, and eye piercing the upper air, like one in a dream. At her first word, there was a profound hush. She spoke in deep tones, which, though not loud, reached every ear in the house.

The second speech by Truth was given at the first annual meeting of the American Equal Rights Association in 1867. Speaking at a time of post–Civil War upheaval, she urges her audience to persist in the cause of women's rights "while things are stirring."

Part I: From Sojourner Truth, speech delivered at the Women's Rights Convention, Akron, Ohio, 1851. *Part II:* From Sojourner Truth, speech delivered at the First Annual Meeting of the American Equal Rights Association, New York, New York, May 9, 1867.

Part I

Well, children, where there is so much racket there must be something out o' kilter. I think that 'twixt the Negroes of the South and the women of the North all a-talking about rights, the white men will be in a fix pretty soon.

But what's all this here talking about? That man over there says that women need to be helped into carriages, and lifted over ditches, and to have the best place everywhere. Nobody ever helps me into carriages, or over mud puddles or gives me any best place *(and raising herself to her full height and her voice to a pitch like rolling thunder, she asked)*, and aren't I a woman? Look at me! Look at my arm! *(And she bared her right arm to the shoulder, showing her tremendous muscular power.)* I have plowed, and planted, and gathered into barns, and no man could head me—and aren't I a woman? I could work as much and eat as much as a man (when I could get it), and bear the lash as well—and aren't I a woman? I have borne thirteen children and seen them almost all sold off into slavery, and when I cried out with a mother's grief, none but Jesus heard—and aren't I a woman? Then they talk about this thing in the head—what's this they call it? *("Intellect," whispered someone near.)* That's it honey. What's that got to do with woman's rights or Negroes' rights? If my cup won't hold but a pint and yours holds a quart, wouldn't you be mean not to let me have my little half-measure full? *(And she pointed her significant finger and sent a keen glance at the minister who had made the argument. The cheering was long and loud.)*

Then that little man in black there, he says women can't have as much rights as man, 'cause Christ wasn't a woman. Where did your Christ come from? *(Rolling thunder could not have stilled that crowd as did those deep, wonderful tones, as she stood there with outstretched arms and eye of fire. Raising her voice still louder, she repeated),* Where did your Christ come from? From God and a woman. Man had nothing to do with him. *(Oh! what a rebuke she gave the little man.)*

(Turning again to another objector, she took up the de-

fense of mother Eve. I cannot follower [sic] her through it all. It was pointed, and witty, and solemn, eliciting at almost every sentence deafening applause; and she ended [sic] by asserting that) If the first woman God ever made was strong enough to turn the world upside down, all alone, these together *(and she glanced her eye over us),* ought to be able to turn it back and get it right side up again; and now they are asking to do it, the men better let them. *(Long-continued cheering.)*

'Bliged to you for hearing on me, and now old Sojourner hasn't got anything more to say.

Part II

My friends, I am rejoiced that you are glad, but I don't know how you will feel when I get through. I come from another field—the country of the slave. They have got their liberty—so much good luck to have slavery partially destroyed; not entirely. I want it root and branch destroyed. Then we will all be free indeed. I feel that if I have to answer for the deeds done in my body just as much as a man, I have a right to have just as much as a man. There is a great stir about colored men getting their rights, but not a word about the colored women; and if colored men get their rights, and not colored women get theirs, you see the colored men will be masters over the women, and it will be just as bad as it was before. So I am for keeping the thing going while things are stirring; because if we wait till it is still, it will take a great while to get it going again. White women are a great deal smarter, and know more than colored women, while colored women do not know scarcely anything. They go out washing, which is about as high as a colored woman gets, and their men go about idle, strutting up and down; and when the women come home, they ask for their money and take it all, and then scold because there is no food. I want you to consider on that, chil'n. I call you chil'n; you are somebody's chil'n, and I am old enough to be mother of all that is here.

I want women to have their rights. In the courts women have no right, no voice; nobody speaks for them. I wish woman to have her voice there among the pettifoggers. If it is not a fit place for women, it is unfit for men to be there.

I am above eighty years old; it is about time for me to be going. I have been forty years a slave and forty years free, and would be here forty years more to have equal rights for all. I suppose I am kept here because something remains for me to do; I suppose I am yet to help break the chain.

I have done a great deal of work; as much as a man, but did not get so much pay. I used to work in the field and bind grain, keeping up with the cradler; but men doing no more, got twice as much pay. So with the German women. They work in the field and do as much work, but do not get the pay. We do as much, we eat as much, we want as much.

I suppose I am about the only colored woman that goes about to speak for the rights of the colored woman. I want to keep the thing stirring, now that the ice is cracked. What we want is a little money. You men know that you get as much again as women when you write, or for what you do. When we get our rights, we shall not have to come to you for money, for then we shall have money enough in our own pockets; and may be you will ask us for money. But help us now until we get it. It is a good consolation to know that when we have got this battle once fought we shall not be coming to you any more.

You have been having our right so long, that you think, like a slave-holder, that you own us. I know that it is hard for one who has held the reins for so long to give up; it cuts like a knife. It will feel all the better when it closes up again. I have been in Washington about three years, seeing about these colored people. Now colored men have a right to vote. There ought to be equal rights more than ever, since colored people have got their freedom.

I am going to talk several times while I am here; so now I will do a little singing. I have not heard any singing since I came here.

(Accordingly, suiting the action to the word, Sojourner sang,) We are going home. There, children, *(said she,)* in heaven we shall rest from all our labors; first do all we have to do here. There I am determined to go, not to stop short of that beautiful place, and I do not mean to stop till I get there, and meet you there, too.

GREAT
SPEECHES
IN
HISTORY

Voices from the Suffrage Movement

On Being Arrested for Voting

Susan B. Anthony

So closely is Susan B. Anthony associated with the achievement of women's suffrage that the Nineteenth Amendment, which gives women the right to vote, is often called the "Susan B. Anthony amendment." Like other women's rights leaders of her time, Susan B. Anthony traveled the nation rallying support for suffrage; however, Anthony's extraordinary zeal for the cause made her a celebrity in her own time and forever afterwards.

In collaboration with Elizabeth Cady Stanton, Anthony called for a constitutional amendment that would guarantee the right to vote for all Americans. In contrast to other activists, who favored an approach by which individual states would implement legislation allowing women the right to vote, Anthony and Stanton demanded that the federal government ensure women's suffrage.

In the speech below, Anthony argues that if women are people, then by definition they are citizens; if they are citizens, they deserve the basic rights accorded by the Constitution. Anthony maintains that a Fifteenth Amendment granting women's suffrage is necessary because the government has a responsibility to clearly define and protect the rights of its citizens.

Anthony wrote the following speech shortly after her indictment for voting. In what was one of the few acts of civil disobedience practiced by American suffragists, Anthony cast a ballot in the 1872 presidential election and was subsequently arrested for violating federal law. She was convicted by a judge and fined one hundred dollars,

From Susan B. Anthony, "Is It a Crime for a U.S. Citizen to Vote?" speech delivered many times during 1872–73.

which she refused to pay. Some say that this famous speech, delivered over forty times in different New York districts, made the judge reluctant to impose a harsh sentence on Anthony.

Friends and Fellow-citizens: I stand before you to-night, under indictment for the alleged crime of having voted at the last Presidential election, without having a lawful right to vote. It shall be my work this evening to prove to you that in thus voting, I not only committed no crime, but, instead, simply exercised my *citizen's right*, guaranteed to me and all United States citizens by the National Constitution, beyond the power of any State to deny.

Our democratic-republican government is based on the idea of the natural right of every individual member thereof to a voice and a vote in making and executing the laws. We assert the province of government to be to secure the people in the enjoyment of their unalienable rights. We throw to the winds the old dogma that governments can give rights. Before governments were organized, no one denies that each individual possessed the right to protect his own life, liberty and property. And when 100 or 1,000,000 people enter into a free government, they do not barter away their natural rights; they simply pledge themselves to protect each other in the enjoyment of them, through prescribed judicial and legislative tribunals. They agree to abandon the methods of brute force in the adjustment of their differences, and adopt those of civilization.

Nor can you find a word in any of the grand documents left us by the fathers that assumes for government the power to create or to confer rights. The Declaration of Independence, the United States Constitution, the constitutions of the several States and the organic laws of the territories, all alike propose to protect the people in the exercise of their God-given rights. Not one of them pretends to bestow rights.

All men are created equal, and endowed by their Creator with certain unalienable rights. Among these are life, liberty and the pursuit of happiness. That to secure these, governments are instituted among men, deriving their just powers from the consent of the governed.

Here is no shadow of government authority over rights, nor exclusion of any class from their full and equal enjoyment. Here is pronounced the right of all men, and "consequently," as the Quaker preacher said, "of all women," to a voice in the government. And here, in this very first paragraph of the Declaration, is the assertion of the natural right of all to the ballot; for, how can "the consent of the governed" be given, if the right to vote be denied. Again:

That whenever any form of government becomes destructive of these ends, it is the right of the people to alter or abolish it, and to institute a new government, laying its foundation on such principles, and organizing its powers in such forms as to them shall seem most likely to effect their safety and happiness.

A Disfranchised Class

Surely, the right of the whole people to vote is here clearly implied. For however destructive to their happiness this government might become, a disfranchised class could neither alter nor abolish it, nor institute a new one, except by the old brute force method of insurrection and rebellion. One-half of the people of this nation to-day are utterly powerless to blot from the statute books an unjust law, or to write there a new and a just one. The women, dissatisfied as they are with this form of government, that enforces taxation without representation—that compels them to obey laws to which they have never given their consent—that imprisons and hangs them without a trial by a jury of their peers, that robs them, in marriage, of the custody of their own persons, wages and children—are this half of the people left wholly at the mercy of the other half, in direct violation of the spirit and letter of the declarations of the framers of this government, every one of which was based on the immutable principle of equal rights to all. By those declarations, kings, priests, popes, aristocrats, were all alike dethroned, and placed on a common level, politically, with the lowliest born subject or serf. By them, too, men, as such, were deprived of their divine right to rule, and placed on a political level with women. By the practice of those declarations all class and caste distinction will be abolished; and slave, serf, plebeian, wife, woman, all alike, bound from their subject position to the proud platform of equality.

The preamble of the Federal Constitution says:

We, the people of the United States, in order to form a more perfect union, establish justice, insure *domestic* tranquility, provide for the common defence, promote the general welfare and secure the blessings of liberty to ourselves and our posterity, do ordain and establish this constitution for the United States of America.

It was we, the people, not we, the white male citizens, nor yet we, the male citizens; but we, the whole people, who formed this Union. And we formed it, not to give the blessings of liberty, but to secure them; not to the half of ourselves and the half of our posterity, but to the whole people—women as well as men. And it is downright mockery to talk to women of their enjoyment of the blessings of liberty while they are denied the use of the only means of securing them provided by this democratic-republican government—the ballot. . . .

Defining Citizenship

Though the words persons, people, inhabitants, electors, citizens, are all used indiscriminately in the national and state constitutions, there was always a conflict of opinion, prior to the war, as to whether they were synonymous terms, as for instance: "No *person* shall be a *representative* who shall not have been seven years a *citizen,* and who shall not, when elected, be an *inhabitant* of that State in which he is chosen. No *person* shall be a senator who shall not have been a *citizen* of the United States, and an *inhabitant* of that State in which he is chosen."

But, whatever room there was for a doubt, under the old regime, the adoption of the fourteenth amendment settled that question forever, in its first sentence: "All persons born or naturalized in the United States and subject to the jurisdiction thereof, are citizens of the United States and of the

State wherein they reside."

And the second settles the equal status of all persons—all citizens: "No State shall make or enforce any law which shall abridge the privileges or immunities of citizens; nor shall any State deprive any person of life, liberty or property, without due process of law, nor deny to any person within its jurisdiction the equal protection of the laws."

The only question left to be settled, now, is: Are women persons? And I hardly believe any of our opponents will have the hardihood to say they are not. Being persons, then, women are citizens, and no State has a right to make any new law, or to enforce any old law, that shall abridge their privileges or immunities. Hence, every discrimination against women in the constitutions and laws of the several States, is to-day null and void, precisely as is every one against negroes.

Is the right to vote one of the privileges or immunities of citizens? I think the disfranchised ex-rebels, and the ex-state prisoners will all agree with me, that it is not only one of them, but the one without which all the others are nothing. Seek first the kingdom of the ballot, and all things else shall be given thee, is the political injunction.

Webster, Worcester and Bouvier [dictionaries] all define citizen to be a person, in the United States, entitled to vote and hold office.

Prior to the adoption of the thirteenth amendment, by which slavery was forever abolished, and black men transformed from property to persons, the judicial opinions of the country had always been in harmony with these definitions. To be a person was to be a citizen, and to be a citizen was to be a voter.

Associate Justice Bushrod Washington, in defining the privileges and immunities of the citizen, more than fifty years ago, said: "they included all such privileges as were fundamental in their nature. And among them is the right to exercise the elective franchise, and to hold office."

Even the "Dred Scott" decision,[1] pronounced by the abo-

---

1. Supreme Court Decision of 1857, *Scott v. Sandford*, which held that Congress had no power to prohibit slavery in the territories and that the Missouri Compromise was unconstitutional, a decision that inflamed the sectional controversy leading to the Civil War.

litionists and Republicans infamous, because it virtually declared "black men had no rights white men were bound to respect," gave this true and logical conclusion, that to be one of the people was to be a citizen and a voter.

Chief Judge [Peter Vivian] Daniels [sic] said: "There is not, it is believed, to be found in the theories of writers on government, or in any actual experiment heretofore tried, an exposition of the term citizen, which has not been considered as conferring the actual possession and enjoyment of the perfect right of acquisition and enjoyment of an entire equality of privileges, civil and political."

Associate Justice [Roger Brooke] Taney said: "The words 'people of the United States,' and 'citizens,' are synonymous terms, and mean the same thing. They both describe the political body, who, according to our republican institutions, form the sovereignty, and who hold the power and conduct the government, through their representatives. They are what we familiarly call the sovereign people, and every citizen is one of this people, and a constituent member of this sovereignty.". . .

The Need for Federal Protection

Clearly, . . . the national government must not only define the rights of citizens, but it must stretch out its powerful hand and protect them in every State in this Union.

But if you will insist that the fifteenth amendment's emphatic interdiction against robbing United States citizens of their right to vote, "on account of race, color, or previous condition of servitude," is a recognition of the right, either of the United States, or any State, to rob citizens of that right, for any or all other reasons, I will prove to you that the class of citizens for which I now plead, and to which I belong, may be, and are, by all the principles of our government, and many of the laws of the States, included under the term "previous condition of servitude."

First.—The married women and their legal status. What is servitude? "The condition of a slave." What is a slave? "A person who is robbed of the proceeds of his labor; a person who is subject to the will of another."

By the law of Georgia, South Carolina, and all the States

of the South, the negro had no right to the custody and control of his person. He belonged to his master. If he was disobedient, the master had the right to use correction. If the negro didn't like the correction, and attempted to run away, the master had a right to use coercion to bring him back.

By the law of every State in this union to-day, North as well as South, the married woman has no right to the custody and control of her person. The wife belongs to her husband; and if she refuses obedience to his will, he may use moderate correction, and if she doesn't like his moderate correction, and attempts to leave his "bed and board," the husband may use moderate coercion to bring her back. The little word "moderate," you see, is the saving clause for the wife, and would doubtless be overstepped should her offended husband administer his correction with the "cat-o'-nine-tails," or accomplish his coercion with blood-hounds.

Again, the slave had no right to the earnings of his hands, they belonged to his master; no right to the custody of his children, they belonged to his master; no right to sue or be sued, or testify in the courts. If he committed a crime, it was the master who must sue or be sued.

In many of the States there has been special legislation, giving to married women the right to property inherited, or received by bequest, or earned by the pursuit of any avocation outside of the home; also, giving her the right to sue and be sued in matters pertaining to such separate property; but not a single State of this Union has ever secured the wife in the enjoyment of her right to the joint ownership of the joint earnings of the marriage copartnership. And since, in the nature of things, the vast majority of married women never earn a dollar, by work outside of their families, nor inherit a dollar from their fathers, it follows that from the day of their marriage to the day of the death of their husbands, not one of them ever has a dollar, except it shall please her husband to *let* her have it.

In some of the States, also, there have been laws passed giving to the mother a joint right with the father in the guardianship of the children. But twenty years ago, when our woman's rights movement commenced, by the laws of the State of New York, and all the States, the father had the sole custody and control of the children. No matter if he were a brutal, drunken libertine, he had the legal right without the mother's consent, to apprentice her sons to rumsellers, or her daughters to brothel keepers. He could even will away an unborn child, to some other person than the mother. And in many of the States the law still prevails, and the mothers are still utterly powerless under the common law.

I doubt if there is, to-day, a State in this Union where a married woman can sue or be sued for slander of character, and until quite recently there was not one in which she could sue or be sued for injury of person. However damaging to the wife's reputation any slander may be, she is wholly powerless to institute legal proceedings against her accuser, unless her husband shall join with her; and how often have we heard of the husband conspiring with some outside barbarian to blast the good name of his wife? A married woman cannot testify in courts in cases of joint interest with her husband. A good farmer's wife near Earlville, Ill., who had all the rights she wanted, went to a dentist of the village and had a full set of false teeth, both upper and under. The dentist pronounced them an admirable fit, and the wife declared they gave her fits to wear them; that she could neither chew nor talk with them in her mouth. The dentist sued the husband; his counsel brought the wife as witness; the judge ruled her off the stand, saying "a married woman cannot be a witness in matters of joint interest between herself and her husband." Think of it, ye good wives, the false teeth in your mouths are joint interest with your husbands, about which you are legally incompetent to speak!! If in our frequent and shocking railroad accidents a married woman is injured in her person, in nearly all of the States, it is her husband who must sue the company, and it is to her husband that the damages, if there are any, will be awarded. In Ashfield, Mass., supposed to be the most advanced of any State in the Union in all things, humanitarian as well as intellectual, a married woman was severely injured by a

Susan B. Anthony

defective sidewalk. Her husband sued the corporation and re-covered $13,000 damages. And those $13,000 belong to him *bona fide;* and whenever that unfortunate wife wishes a dollar of it to supply her needs she must ask her husband for it; and if the man be of a narrow, selfish, niggardly nature, she will have to hear him say, every time, "What have you done, my dear, with the twenty-five cents I gave you yesterday?" Isn't such a position, I ask you, humiliating enough to be called "servitude?" That husband, as would any other husband, in nearly every State of this Union, sued and obtained damages for the loss of the services of his wife, precisely as the master, under the old slave regime, would have done, had his slave been thus injured, and precisely as he himself would have done had it been his ox, cow or horse instead of his wife. . . .

Thus may all married women, wives and widows, by the laws of the several States, be technically included in the fifteenth amendment's specification of "condition of servitude," present or previous. And not only married women, but I will also prove to you that by all the great fundamental principles of our free government, the entire womanhood of the nation is in a "condition of servitude" as surely as were our revolutionary fathers when they rebelled against old King George.[2] Women are taxed without representation, governed without their consent, tried, convicted and punished without a jury of their peers. And is all this tyranny any less humiliating and degrading to women under our democratic-republican government to-day than it was to men under their aristocratic, monarchical government one hundred years ago? There is not an utterance of old John Adams, John Hancock or Patrick Henry, but finds a living response in the soul of every intelligent, patriotic woman of the nation. Bring to me a common-sense woman property holder, and I will show you one whose soul is fired with all the indignation of 1776 every time the tax-gatherer presents himself at her door. You will not find one such but feels her condition of servitude as galling as did James Otis when he said:[3]

2. George III (1738–1820), king of Great Britain and Ireland (1760–1820).   3. James Otis (1725–83) led the radical political wing of the colonial opposition to British measures and was head of the Massachusetts committee of correspondence.

The very act of taxing exercised over those who are not represented appears to me to be depriving them of one of their most essential rights, and if continued, seems to be in effect an entire disfranchisement of every civil right. For, what one civil right is worth a rush after a man's property is subject to be taken from him at pleasure without his consent? If a man is not his own assessor in person, or by deputy, his liberty is gone, or he is wholly at the mercy of others.

What was the three-penny tax on tea, or the paltry tax on paper and sugar to which our revolutionary fathers were subjected, when compared with the taxation of the women of this republic? The orphaned Pixley sisters, six dollars a day, and even the women, who are proclaiming the tyranny of our taxation without representation, from city to city throughout the country, are often compelled to pay a tax for the poor privilege of defending our rights. And again, to show that disfranchisement was precisely the slavery of which the fathers complained, allow me to cite to you old Ben. Franklin, who in those olden times was admitted to be good authority, not merely in domestic economy, but in political as well; he said:

Every man of the commonalty [sic], except infants, insane persons and criminals, is, of common right and the law of God, a freeman and entitled to the free enjoyment of liberty. That liberty or freedom consists in having an actual share in the appointment of those who are to frame the laws, and who are to be the guardians of every man's life, property and peace. For the all of one man is as dear to him as the all of another; and the poor man has an equal right, but more need to have representatives in the Legislature than the rich one. That they who have no voice or vote in the electing of representatives, do not enjoy liberty, but are absolutely enslaved to those who have votes and their representatives; for to be enslaved is to have governors whom other men have set over us, and to be subject to laws made by the representatives of others, without having had representatives of our own to give consent in our behalf.

Suppose I read it with the feminine gender:

That women who have no voice nor vote in the electing of

representatives, do not enjoy liberty, but are absolutely enslaved to men who have votes and their representatives; for to be enslaved is to have governors whom men have set over us, and to be subject to the laws made by the representatives of men, without having representatives of our own to give consent in our behalf.

And yet one more authority; that of Thomas Paine, than whom not one of the Revolutionary patriots more able vindicated the principles upon which our government is founded:

> The right of voting for representatives is the primary right by which other rights are protected. To take away this right is to reduce man to a state of slavery; for slavery consists in being subject to the will of another; and he that has not a vote in the election of representatives is in this case. The proposal, therefore, to disfranchise any class of men is as criminal as the proposal to take away property.

Is anything further needed to prove woman's condition of servitude sufficiently orthodox to entitle her to the guarantees of the fifteenth amendment?

Freedom Without the Ballot Is Mockery

Is there a man who will not agree with me, that to talk of freedom without the ballot, is mockery—is slavery—to the women of this Republic, precisely as New England's orator Wendell Phillips, at the close of the late war, declared it to be to the newly emancipated black men?. . .

We no longer petition Legislature or Congress to give us the right to vote. We appeal to the women everywhere to exercise their too long neglected "citizen's right to vote." We appeal to the inspectors of election everywhere to receive the votes of all United States citizens as it is their duty to do. We appeal to United States commissioners and marshals to arrest the inspectors who reject the names and votes of United States citizens, as it is their duty to do, and leave those alone who, like our eighth ward inspectors, perform their duties faithfully and well.

We ask the juries to fail to return verdicts of "guilty"

against honest, law-abiding, tax-paying United States citizens for offering their votes at our elections. Or against intelligent, worthy young men, inspectors of elections, for receiving and counting such citizens' votes.

We ask the judges to render true and unprejudiced opinions of the law, and wherever there is room for a doubt to give its benefit on the side of liberty and equal rights to women, remembering that "the true rule of interpretation under our national Constitution, especially since its amendments, is that anything for human rights is constitutional, everything against human rights is unconstitutional."

And it is on this line that we propose to fight our battle for the ballot—all peaceably, but nevertheless persistently through to complete triumph, when all United States citizens shall be recognized as equals before the law.

Why Women Need the Ballot

Frances D. Gage

During the late nineteenth century, women's rights and the abolition of slavery were closely linked. Most advocates of women's rights were first passionate abolitionists. However, the discrimination they met within abolitionist organizations—whose officials sometimes refused to allow women to speak publicly—became a major impetus for the women's rights movement. Women's rights leaders were also some of the most vocal supporters of temperance. They argued that alcohol was a destructive force because it induced men to abdicate their responsibilities toward their wives and children.

Frances D. Gage was an outspoken activist for all three of these causes. While raising eight children, Gage educated herself by reading and began to write newspaper articles voicing her opinions. She eventually became the most prominent women's rights activist in the state of Ohio. During the Civil War, Gage assisted the abolition movement by serving as the superintendent of a camp of 500 freed slaves on Parris Island, South Carolina.

As is evident from the following speech, delivered at the first anniversary of the American Equal Rights Association, Gage was an engaging speaker who used humor to illustrate her points. This speech articulates the relationship between the causes of women's rights, abolition, and temperance. Gage was a strong believer that women's suffrage would enable the passage of temperance laws, which would improve the morality of society.

From Frances D. Gage, speech delivered at the First Annual Meeting of the American Equal Rights Association, New York, New York, May 9, 1867.

We have been talking about the right to the ballot. Why do we want it? What does it confer? What will it give us? We closed our argument at three o'clock to-day by a discussion whether the women of this country and the colored men of this country wanted the ballot. I said that it was a libel on the womanhood of this country, to say they do not want it; and I repeat that assertion. Woman may say in public that she does not want it, because it is unpopular and unfashionable for her to want it; but when you tell her what the ballot can do, she will always answer you that she wants it. Why do we want it? Because it is right, and because there are wrongs in the community that can be righted in no other way.

After the discussions we have had to-night, I want to turn to a fresh subject. Last evening I attended the meeting of the National Temperance Association at Cooper Institute. A great audience was assembled there, to listen to the arguments against the most gigantic evil that now pervades the American Republic. Men took the position that only a prohibitory law could put an end to the great evil of intemperance. New York has its two hundred millions of invested capital to sell death and destruction to the men of this country who are weak enough to purchase. There are eight thousand licensed liquor establishments in this city, to drag down humanity. It was asserted there by Wendell Phillips that intemperance had its root in our Saxon blood, that demanded a stimulus; and he argued from that standpoint. If intemperance has its root in the Saxon blood, that demands a stimulus, why is it that the womanhood of this nation is not at the grog-shops to-day? Are women not Saxons? . . . I was at Harrisburg, a few days ago, at the State Temperance Convention. Horace Greeley asserted that there was progress upon the subject of temperance; and he went back to the time when ardent spirits were drank in the household, when every table had its decanter, and the wife, children and husband drank together. Now, said he, it is a rare thing to find the dram-bottle in the home. It has been put out. But what put the dram-bottle out of the home? It was put out because the education and refinement and power of woman became so strong in the home, that she said, "It must go out; we can't have it here." (*Applause.*) Then the voters of the United States, the white male citizens, went to work and licensed these nuisances that could not be in the home, at all the corners of the streets. I demand the ballot for woman to-day, that she may vote down these nuisances, the dram-shops, there also, as she drove them out of the home. (*Applause.*)

A Picture of the "White Male Citizen"

What privilege does the vote give to the "white male citizen" of the United States? Did you ever analyze a voter—hold him up and see what he was? Shall I give you a picture of him? Not as my friend Parker Pillsbury has drawn the picture tonight will I draw it. What is the "white male citizen"—the voter in the Republic of the United States? More than any potentate or any king in all Europe. Louis Napoleon dares not walk the streets of his own city without his bodyguard around him, with their bayonets. The Czar of Russia is afraid for his own life among his people. Kings and potentates are always afraid; but the "free white male citizen" of the United States, with the ballot in his hand, goes where he lists, does what he pleases. He owns himself, his earnings, his genius, his talent, his eloquence, his power, all there is of him. All that God has given him is his, to do with as he pleases, subject to no power but such laws as have an equal bearing upon every other man in like circumstances, and responsible to no power but his own conscience and his God. He builds colleges; he lifts up humanity or he casts it down. He is the lawgiver, the maker, as it were, of the nation. His single vote may turn the destiny of the whole Republic for good or ill. There is no link in the chain of human possibilities that can add one single power to the "white male citizen" of America.

Now we ask that you shall put into the hands of every human soul this same power to go forward and do good works wherever it can. The country has rung within the last few days because one colored girl, with a little black blood in her veins, has been cast out of the Pittsburg Methodist College. It ought to ring until such a thing shall be impossible. But when Cambridge, and Yale, and Union, and Lansing, and all the other institutions of the country, West Point included, aided by national patronage, shut out every woman and every colored man in the land, who has anything to say? There is not a single college instituted by the original government patronage of lands to public schools and colleges, that allows a woman to set her foot inside of its walls as a student. Is this no injustice? Is it no wrong?

Women's "Weakness"

When men stand upon the public platform and deliver elaborate essays on women and their right of suffrage, they talk about their weakness, their devotion to fashion and idleness. What else have they given women to do? Almost every profession in the land is filled by men; every college sends forth the men to fill the highest places. When the law said that no married woman should do business in her own name, sue or be sued, own property, own herself or her earnings, what had she to do? That laid the foundation for precisely the state of things you see to-day.

But I deny that, as a class, the women of America, black or white, are idle. We are always busy. What have we done? Look over this audience, go out upon your streets, go through the world where you will, and every human soul you meet is the work of woman. She has given it life; she has educated it, whether for good or evil. She it is that must lie at the foundation of your country, because God gave her the holiest mission ever laid upon the heart of a human soul—the mission of the mother.

We are told that home is woman's sphere. So it is, and man's sphere, too; for I tell you that that is a poor home which has not in it a man to feel that it is the most sacred place he knows. If duty requires him to go out into the world and fight its battles, who blames him, or puts a ban upon him? Men complain that woman does not love home now, that she is not satisfied with her mission. I answer that this discontent arises out of the one fact, that you have attempted to mold seventeen millions of human souls in one shape, and make them all do one thing. Take away your restrictions, open all doors, leave women at liberty to go where they will. As old Sojourner Truth said twenty years ago, at the first

Women's Rights Convention in Ohio, "Leave them where God left them, with their inalienable rights," and they will adjust themselves to their convictions of their duties, their responsibilities, and their powers, and society will find harmony within itself. The caged bird forgets how to build its nest. The wing of the eagle is as strong to soar to the sun as that of her mate, who never says to her, "back, feeble one, to your nest, and there brood in dull inactivity until I give you permission to leave!" But when her duties called her there, who ever found her unfaithful to her trust? The foot of the wild roe is as strong and swift in the race as that of her antlered companion. She goes by his side, she feeds in the same pasture, drinks from the same running brook, but is ever true also to her maternal duties and cares.

If we are a nation of imbeciles, if womanhood is weak, it is the laws and customs of society which have made us what we are. If you want health, strength, energy, force, temperance, purity, honesty, deal justly with the mothers of this country; then they will give you nobler and stronger men than higgling politicians, or the grog-shop emissaries that buy up the votes of your manhood.

Why is it that Republicans are so weak and wavering today? There is a law upon the statute book of every southern State that the child shall follow the condition of the mother. There is a law in the physical code of humanity, written by the finger of the Almighty, that never was and never will be repealed, that the child shall follow the condition of the mother. You have never taught the women of this country the sacredness of freedom. You have never called out the mother to generous action. You have never said to the motherhood of this country, "Upon you rests the responsibility of making the Republic what it should be. We invest you with the power; now assume that responsibility and act upon it, or we shall call you to account for your neglect of duty."

It has been charged upon woman that she does nothing well. What have you given us to do well? What freedom have you given us to act independently and earnestly? When I was in San Domingo, I found a little colony of American colored people that went over there in 1825. They retained their American customs, and especially their little American church, outside of the Catholic, which overspread the whole country. In an obscure room in an old ruin they sung the old hymns, and lived the old life of the United States. I asked how this thing was, and they answered that among those that went over so long ago were a few from Chester County, Penn., who were brought up among the Quakers, and had learned to read. Wherever a mother had learned to read, she had educated all her children so that they could read; but wherever there was a mother that could not read, that family had lapsed off from the old customs of the past.

Give us education. When we have a right to vote, there will not be a school-door in the United States shut to woman. When we have the right to vote, I believe that the womanhood that demanded that the dram-bottle should go out of the home, will demand that the dram-bottle shall be put away from among men. She will say, You have no right to take poison, and make my home a discomfort, or destroy the greenbacks, which should be the mutual possession of the household, by lighting your cigar. She will tell the world, under the new regime, that it is not the Saxon blood that demands a stimulant; but in the new morality it will be as wicked for a man to be drunken as for a woman to be drunken—as disreputable for a man to be licentious as for a woman to be licentious—as wicked and perverse for a man to go down to the lower depths of iniquity and folly as for a woman. And the great law uttered upon Sinai amid its thunders, will again be remembered, and will apply as much to man as to woman. Now, it is not so. One code of morality governs the voter, another the woman. As the slaveholder enacted laws that made his own vices crimes in the slave, so men enact laws that make their vices crimes in woman. And this is why we want suffrage for woman.

Taking Our Position as Human Beings

I ask the ballot, not because of its individual advantage to myself, but because I know and feel that individual rights, guaranteed to every citizen, must harmonize the world, if there is any power to do it this side of heaven. And so, not quite eighty years old, as old Sojourner said she was, but standing upon the brink of threescore, having looked this question in the face from my girlhood up—having labored in almost every vocation in life that falls to the lot of womanhood, as a worker on the farm, a worker in the household, a wife, a mother, a seamstress, a cook—and I tell you, my friends, that I can make better biscuit than I can lectures—as one who has tried to study what is for the best interest of society, I ask you candidly to survey this subject in all its bearings. Why may we not take our position as human beings enjoying all the privileges which the Creator bestowed, without restriction other than falls upon every other human being in the community?

A friend of mine, writing from Charleston the other day, just after the ballot went down there, says that he was told by a colored man, "I met my old master, and he bowed so low to me I didn't hardly know which was the negro and which was the white man." When we hold the ballot, we shall stand just there. Men will forget to tell us that politics are degrading. They will bow low, and actually respect the women to whom they now talk platitudes; and silly flatteries, sparkling eyes, rosy cheeks, pearly teeth, ruby lips, the soft and delicate hands of refinement and beauty, will not be the burden of their song; but the strength, the power, the energy, the force, the intellect and the nerve, which the womanhood of this country will bring to bear, and which will infuse itself through all the ranks of society, must make all its men and women wiser and better. (*Applause.*)

The Solitude of Self: An Argument for Women's Suffrage

Elizabeth Cady Stanton

Before the Civil War, the idea that women deserved the right to vote was highly controversial, even within the women's rights movement itself. Many women who supported women's rights felt that suffrage was too daunting a goal, and focused instead on more manageable reforms such as changes to unjust marriage and property laws. Elizabeth Cady Stanton, however, recognized from the beginning that voting rights would be the women's rights movement's most crucial endeavor. Government's refusal to allow women the vote, she argued, was essentially the refusal to recognize them as human beings.

In 1867, Stanton mounted the most vigorous universal suffrage campaign in history, called the National Protection for National Citizens. Working closely with Susan B. Anthony and Matilda Joslyn Gage, she petitioned Congress for a women's suffrage amendment. Unlike many other suffragists of the time, Stanton was adamant that women's right to vote should be mandated by federal law.

Stanton's speech, "The Solitude of Self," given in 1892 to the House Committee on the Judiciary, the Senate Committee, and the National American Woman's Suffrage Association, was the climax of her oratorical career and is considered to be the most eloquent discussion of the humanistic philosophy underlying women's rights. In this speech, Stanton argues that because all individuals are ultimately left to their own devices for survival, they should

From Elizabeth Cady Stanton, "The Solitude of Self," speech delivered at the U.S. House of Representatives Committee on the Judiciary, January 18, 1892.

all be accorded the same rights. She maintains that denying women the right to vote prevents them from attaining
full development as human beings. Age seventy-six when
she first delivered the speech, Stanton was described as
"looking as if she should be the Lord Chief Justice with
her white hair puffed all over her head, and her amiable
and intellectual face marked with lines of wisdom."

T he point I wish plainly to bring before you on this occasion is the individuality of each human soul; our
Protestant idea, the right of individual conscience and
judgment; our republican idea, individual citizenship. In discussing the rights of woman, we are to consider, first, what
belongs to her as an individual, in a world of her own, the arbiter of her own destiny, an imaginary Robinson Crusoe,
with her woman Friday on a solitary island. Her rights under
such circumstances are to use all her faculties for her own
safety and happiness.

Secondly, if we consider her as a citizen, as a member of
a great nation, she must have the same rights as all other
members, according to the fundamental principles of our
government.

Thirdly, viewed as a woman, an equal factor in civilization, her rights and duties are still the same; individual happiness and development.

Fourthly, it is only the incidental relations of life, such as
mother, wife, sister, daughter, that may involve some special
duties and training. In the usual discussion in regard to
woman's sphere, such men as Herbert Spencer, Frederic Harrison and Grant Allen,[1] uniformly subordinate her rights and
duties as an individual, as a citizen, as a woman, to the necessities of these incidental relations, neither of which a large
class of women may ever assume. In discussing the sphere of

1. Herbert Spencer (1820–1903), English philosopher who applied the theory of
evolution to all life; Frederic Harrison (1931–99), jurist, historian, sociologist, and
leader of English positivism; Grant Allen (1848–99), English author, who wrote on
popular science, known for his novel *The Woman Who Did* (1895), an attack on
the moral double standard.

man, we do not decide his rights as an individual, as a citizen, as a man, by his duties as a father, a husband, a brother or a son, relations he may never fill. Moreover, he would be better fitted for these very relations, and whatever special work he might choose to do to earn his bread, by the complete development of all his faculties as an individual.

Just so with woman. The education that will fit her to discharge the duties in the largest sphere of human usefulness will best fit her for whatever special work she may be compelled to do.

The isolation of every human soul, and the necessity of self-dependence, must give each individual the right to choose his own surroundings.

The strongest reason for giving woman all the opportunities for higher education, for the full development of her faculties, forces of mind and body; for giving her the most enlarged freedom of thought and action; a complete emancipation from all forms of bondage, of custom, dependence, superstition; from all the crippling influences of fear—is the solitude and personal responsibility of her own individual life. The strongest reason why we ask for woman a voice in the government under which she lives; in the religion she is asked to believe; equality in social life, where she is the chief factor; a place in the trades and professions, where she may earn her bread, is because of her birthright to self-sovereignty; because, as an individual, she must rely on herself. No matter how much women prefer to lean, to be protected and supported, nor how much men desire to have them to do so, they must make the voyage of life alone, and for safety in an emergency, they must know something of the laws of navigation. To guide our own craft, we must be captain, pilot, engineer; with chart and compass to stand at the wheel; to watch the winds and waves, and know when to take in the sail, and to read the signs in the firmament over all. It matters not whether the solitary voyager is man or woman; nature, having endowed them equally, leaves them to their own skill and judgment in the hour of danger, and, if not equal to the occasion, alike they perish.

To appreciate the importance of fitting every human soul for independent action, think for a moment of the immeasurable solitude of self. We come into the world alone, unlike all who have gone before us; we leave it alone, under circumstances peculiar to ourselves. No mortal ever has been, no mortal ever will be like the soul just launched on the sea of life. There can never again be just such a combination of prenatal influences; never again just such environments as make up the infancy, youth and manhood of this one. Nature never repeats herself, and the possibilities of one human soul will never be found in another. No one has ever found two blades of ribbon grass alike, and no one will ever find two human beings alike. Seeing, then, what must be the infinite diversity in human character, we can in a measure appreciate the loss to a nation when any large class of the people is uneducated and unrepresented in the government.

The Complete Development of Every Individual

We ask for the complete development of every individual, first, for his own benefit and happiness. In fitting out an army, we give each soldier his own knapsack, arms, powder, his blanket, cup, knife, fork and spoon. We provide alike for all their individual necessities; then each man bears his own burden.

Again, we ask complete individual development for the general good; for the consensus of the competent on the whole round of human interests, on all questions of national life; and here each man must bear his share of the general burden. It is sad to see how soon friendless children are left to bear their own burdens, before they can analyze their feelings; before they can even tell their joys and sorrows, they are thrown on their own resources. The great lesson that nature seems to teach us at all ages is self-dependence, self-protection, self-support. What a touching instance of a child's solitude, of that hunger of the heart for love and recognition, in the case of the little girl who helped to dress a Christmas tree for the children of the family in which she served. On finding there was no present for herself, she slipped away in the darkness and spent the night in an open field sitting on a stone, and when found in the morning was weeping as if her heart would break. No mortal will ever know the thoughts that passed through the mind of that friendless child in the long hours of that cold night, with only the silent stars to keep her company. The mention of her case in the daily papers moved many generous hearts to send her presents, but in the hours of her keenest suffering she was thrown wholly on herself for consolation.

In youth our most bitter disappointments, our brightest hopes and ambitions, are known only to ourselves. Even our friendship and love we never fully share with another; there is something of every passion, in every situation, we conceal. Even so in our triumphs and our defeats. The successful candidate for the presidency, and his opponent, each has a solitude peculiarly his own, and good form forbids either to speak of his pleasure or regret. The solitude of the king on his throne and the prisoner in his cell differs in character and degree, but it is solitude, nevertheless.

The Awful Solitude of Individual Life

We ask no sympathy from others in the anxiety and agony of a broken friendship or shattered love. When death sunders our nearest ties, alone we sit in the shadow of our affliction. Alike amid the greatest triumphs and darkest tragedies of life, we walk alone. On the divine heights of human attainment, eulogized and worshipped as a hero or saint, we stand alone. In ignorance, poverty and vice, as a pauper or criminal, alone we starve or steal; alone we suffer the sneers and rebuffs of our fellows; alone we are hunted and hounded through dark courts and alleys, in by-ways and highways; alone we stand in the judgment seat; alone in the prison cell we lament our crimes and misfortunes; alone we expiate them on the gallows. In hours like these we realize the awful solitude of individual life, its pains, its penalties, its responsibilities; hours in which the youngest and most helpless are thrown on their own resources for guidance and consolation. Seeing, then, that life must ever be a march and a battle, that each soldier must be equipped for his own protection, it is the height of cruelty to rob the individual of a single natural right.

To throw obstacles in the way of a complete education is like putting out the eyes; to deny the rights of property, like cutting off the hands. To deny political equality is to rob the ostracised of all self-respect; of credit in the market place; of recompense in the world of work; of a voice in those who make and administer the law; a choice in the jury before whom they are tried, and in the judge who decides their punishment. Shakespeare's play of "Titus Andronicus" contains a terrible satire on woman's position in the 19th century. Rude men (the play tells us) seized the king's daughter, cut out her tongue, cut off her hands, and then bade her go call for water and wash her hands. What a picture of woman's position! Robbed of her natural rights, handicapped by law and custom at every turn, yet compelled to fight her own battles, and in the emergencies of life to fall back on herself for protection.

The girl of sixteen, thrown on the world to support herself, to make her own place in society, to resist the temptations that surround her and maintain a spotless integrity, must do all this by native force or superior education. She does not acquire this power by being trained to trust others and distrust herself. If she wearies of the struggle, finding it hard work to swim up stream, and allows herself to drift with the current, she will find plenty of company, but not one to share her misery in the hour of her deepest humiliation. If she tries to retrieve her position, to conceal the past, her life is hedged about with fears lest willing hands should tear the veil from what she fain would hide. Young and friendless, *she* knows the bitter solitude of self.

How the little courtesies of life on the surface of society, deemed so important from man towards woman, fade into utter insignificance in view of the deeper tragedies in which she must play her part alone, where no human aid is possible!

The young wife and mother, at the head of some establishment, with a kind husband to shield her from the adverse winds of life, with wealth, fortune and position, has a certain harbor of safety, secure against the ordinary ills of life. But to manage a household, have a desirable influence in society, keep her friends and the affections of her husband, train her children and servants well, she must have rare common sense, wisdom, diplomacy, and a knowledge of human nature. To do all this, she needs the cardinal virtues and the strong points of character that the most successful statesman possesses. An uneducated woman trained to dependence, with no resources in herself, must make a failure of any position in life. But society says women do not need a knowledge of the world, the liberal training that experience in public life must give, all the advantages of collegiate education, but when for the lack of all this, the woman's happiness is wrecked, alone she bears her humiliation; and the solitude of the weak and the ignorant is indeed pitiable. In the wild chase for the prizes of life, they are ground to powder.

Imag[in]e when the pleasures of youth are passed, children grown up, married and gone, the hurry and bustle of life in a measure over, when the hands are weary of active service, when the old arm chair and the fireside are the chosen resorts, then men and women alike must fall back on their own resources. If they cannot find companionship in books, if they have no interest in the vital questions of the hour, no interest in watching the consummation of reforms with which they might have been identified, they soon pass into their dotage. The more fully the faculties of the mind are developed and kept in use, the longer the period of vigor and active interest in all around us continues. If, from a life-long participation in public affairs, a woman feels responsible for the laws regulating our system of education, the discipline of our jails and prisons, the sanitary condition of our private homes, public buildings and thoroughfares, an interest in commerce, finance, our foreign relations, in any or all these questions, her solitude will at least be respectable, and she will not be driven to gossip or scandal for entertainment.

The chief reason for opening to every soul the doors to the whole round of human duties and pleasures is the individual development thus attained, the resources thus provided under all circumstances to mitigate the solitude that at times must come to everyone. I once asked Prince Piotr Alekseyevich Kropotkin, a Russian Nihilist, how he endured his long years in prison, deprived of books, pen, ink and paper. "Ah!" said he, "I thought out many questions in which I had a deep interest. In the pursuit of an idea, I took no note of time. When tired solving knotty problems, I recited all the beautiful passages in prose and verse I had ever learned. I became acquainted with myself, and my own resources. I had a world of my own, a vast empire, that no Russian jailer or Czar could invade." Such is the value of liberal thought and broad culture, when shut off from all human companionship, bringing comfort and sunshine within even the four walls of a prison cell.

As women ofttimes share a similar fate, should they not have all the consolation that the most liberal education can give? Their suffering in the prisons of St. Petersburg; in the long weary marches to Siberia, and in the mines, working side by side with men, surely call for all the self-support that the most exalted sentiments of heroism can give. When suddenly roused at midnight, with the startling cry of "Fire! Fire!" to find the house over their heads in flames, do women wait for men to point the way to safety? And are the men, equally bewildered, and half suffocated with smoke, in a position to do more than try to save themselves? At such times the most timid women have shown a courage and heroism, in saving their husbands and children, that has surprised everybody. Inasmuch, then, as woman shares equally the joys and sorrows of time and eternity, is it not the height of presumption in man to propose to represent her at the ballot box and the throne of grace, to do her voting in the State, her praying in the church, and to assume the position of High Priest at the family altar?

Nothing strengthens the judgment and quickens the conscience like individual responsibility; nothing adds such dignity to character as the recognition of one's self-sovereignty; the right to an equal place, everywhere conceded; a place earned by personal merit, not an artificial attainment by inheritance, wealth, family and position. Seeing, then, that the responsibilities of life rest equally on man and woman, that their destiny is the same, they need the same preparation for time and eternity. The talk of sheltering woman from the fierce storms of life is the sheerest mockery, for they beat on her from every point of the compass, just as they do on man, and with more fatal results, for he has been trained to protect himself, to resist, and to conquer. Such are the facts in human experience, the responsibilities of individual sovereignty. Rich and poor, intelligent and ignorant, wise and foolish, virtuous and vicious, man and woman; it is ever the same, each soul must depend wholly on itself.

Man Cannot Bear Woman's Burdens

Whatever the theories may be of woman's dependence on man, in the supreme moments of her life, he cannot bear her burdens. Alone she goes to the gates of death to give life to every man that is born into the world; no one can share her fears, no one can mitigate her pangs; and if her sorrow is greater than she can bear, alone she passes beyond the gates into the vast unknown.

From the mountain-tops of Judea long ago, a heavenly voice bade his disciples, "Bear ye one another's burdens" [Gal. 6:2]; but humanity has not yet risen to that point of self-sacrifice; and if ever so willing, how few the burdens are that one soul can bear for another! In the highways of Palestine; in prayer and fasting on the solitary mountain-top; in the Garden of Gethsemane; before the judgment-seat of Pilate; betrayed by one of his trusted disciples at his last supper; in his agonies on the cross, even Jesus of Nazareth, in those last sad days on earth, felt the awful solitude of self. Deserted by man, in agony he cries, "My God, my God, why hast thou forsaken me?" [Matt. 27:46; Mark 15:34]. And so it ever must be in the conflicting scenes of life, in the long, weary march, each one walks alone. We may have many friends, love, kindness, sympathy and charity, to smooth our pathway in everyday life, but in the tragedies and triumphs of human experience, each mortal stands alone.

But when all artificial trammels are removed, and women are recognized as individuals, responsible for their own environments, thoroughly educated for all positions in life they may be called to fill; with all the resources in themselves that liberal thought and broad culture can give; guided by their own conscience and judgment, trained to self-protection, by a healthy development of the muscular system, and skill in the use of weapons of defense; and stimulated to self-support by a knowledge of the business world and the pleasure that pecuniary independence must ever give; when women are trained in this way, they will in a measure be fitted for those hours of solitude that come alike to all, whether prepared or otherwise. As in our extremity we must depend on ourselves, the dictates of wisdom point to complete individual development. . . .

We see reason sufficient in the outer conditions of human beings for individual liberty and development, but when we consider the self-dependence of every human soul we see the need of courage, judgment and the exercise of every faculty of mind and body, strengthened and developed by use, in woman as well as man.

Whatever may be said of man's protecting power in ordinary conditions, amid all the terrible disasters by land and sea, in the supreme moments of danger, alone woman must ever meet the horrors of the situation. The Angel of Death even makes no royal pathway for her. Man's love and sympathy enter only into the sunshine of our lives. In that solemn solitude of self, that links us with the immeasurable and the eternal, each soul lives alone forever. A recent writer says:

> I remember once, in crossing the Atlantic, to have gone upon the deck of the ship at midnight, when a dense black cloud enveloped the sky, and the great deep was roaring madly under the lashes of demoniac winds. My feeling was not of danger or fear (which is a base surrender of the immortal soul) but of utter desolation and loneliness; a little speck of life shut in by a tremendous darkness. Again I remember to have climbed the slopes of the Swiss Alps, up beyond the point where vegetation ceases, and the stunted conifers no longer struggle against the unfeeling blasts. Around me lay a huge confusion of rocks, out of which the gigantic ice peaks shot into the measureless blue of the heavens; and again my only feeling was the awful solitude.

And yet, there is a solitude which each and every one of us has always carried with him, more inaccessible than the ice-cold mountains, more profound than the midnight sea; the solitude of self. Our inner being which we call ourself, no eye nor touch of man or angel has ever pierced. It is more hidden than the caves of the gnome; the sacred adytum of the oracle; the hidden chamber of Eleusinian mystery, for to it only Omniscience is permitted to enter.

Such is individual life. Who, I ask you, can take, dare take on himself the rights, the duties, the responsibilities of another human soul?

Militant Suffragists

Emmeline Pankhurst

By 1913, when British suffragist Emmeline Pankhurst gave this speech to a crowd in Hartford, Connecticut, many women were beginning to wonder whether the suffrage movement would ever obtain its goal. Frustrated with the movement's failure to win the ballot for women despite over six decades of work, many suffragists had grown increasingly militant. Some, such as Pankhurst, pledged to achieve women's suffrage by any means necessary.

An ardent feminist whose mother had taken her to suffrage meetings at an early age, Pankhurst was the founder of the Women's Social and Political Union, a women's rights group that adopted tactics of civil disobedience—such as interfering with government meetings and refusing to leave—in its quest for suffrage. Pankhurst was arrested numerous times for her acts of civil disobedience, but her commitment to the cause of suffrage was tireless. In the speech that follows, Pankhurst contends that women must be prepared to use whatever means are available to them—even the sacrifice of their own lives—in order to achieve suffrage. The government is faced with only two alternatives, she writes; either women will be killed, or they will have the right to vote.

I do not come here as an advocate, because whatever position the suffrage movement may occupy in the United States of America, in England it has passed beyond the realm of advocacy and it has entered into the sphere of practical politics. It has become the subject of revolution and civil war, and so to-night I am not here to advocate woman suf-

From Emmeline Pankhurst, "Militant Suffragists," speech delivered at Hartford, Connecticut, November 13, 1913.

frage. American suffragists can do that very well for themselves. I am here as a soldier who has temporarily left the
field of battle in order to explain—it seems strange it should
have to be explained—what civil war is like when civil war
is waged by women. I am not only here as a soldier temporarily absent from the field of battle; I am here—and that,
I think, is the strangest part of my coming—I am here as a
person who, according to the law courts of my country, it has
been decided, is of no value to the community at all; and I am
adjudged because of my life to be a dangerous person, under
sentence of penal servitude in a convict prison. So you see
there is some special interest in hearing so unusual a person
address you. I dare say, in the minds of many of you—you
will perhaps forgive me this personal touch—that I do not
look either very like a soldier or very like a convict, and yet
I am both.

It would take too long to trace the course of militant
methods as adopted by women, because it is about eight
years since the word militant was first used to describe what
we were doing; it is about eight years since the first militant
action was taken by women. It was not militant at all, except
that it provoked militancy on the part of those who were opposed to it. When women asked questions in political meetings and failed to get answers, they were not doing anything
militant. To ask questions at political meetings is an acknowledged right of all people who attend public meetings;
certainly in my country, men have always done it, and I hope
they do it in America, because it seems to me that if you allow people to enter your legislatures without asking them
any questions as to what they are going to do when they get
there you are not exercising your citizen rights and your citizen duties as you ought. At any rate in Great Britain it is a
custom, a time-honored one, to ask questions of candidates
for Parliament and ask questions of members of the government. No man was ever put out of a public meeting for asking a question until Votes for Women came onto the political
horizon. The first people who were put out of a political
meeting for asking questions, were women; they were brutally ill-used; they found themselves in jail before twenty-four
hours had expired. But instead of the newspapers, which are

largely inspired by the politicians, putting militancy and the reproach of militancy, if reproach there is, on the people who had assaulted the women, they actually said it was the women who were militant and very much to blame.

It was not the speakers on the platform who would not answer them, who were to blame, or the ushers at the meeting; it was the poor women who had had their bruises and their knocks and scratches, and who were put into prison for doing precisely nothing but holding a protest meeting in the street after it was all over. However, we were called militant for doing that, and we were quite willing to accept the name, because militancy for us is time-honored; you have the church militant and in the sense of spiritual militancy we were very militant indeed. We were determined to press this question of the enfranchisement of the women to the point where we were no longer to be ignored by the politicians as had been the case for about fifty years, during which time women had patiently used every means open to them to win their political enfranchisement.

Enough of Sympathy

Experience will show you that if you really want to get anything done, it is not so much a matter of whether you alienate sympathy; sympathy is a very unsatisfactory thing if it is not practical sympathy. It does not matter to the practical suffragist whether she alienates sympathy that was never of any use to her. What she wants is to get something practical done, and whether it is done out of sympathy or whether it is done out of fear, or whether it is done because you want to be comfortable again and not be worried in this way, doesn't particularly matter so long as you get it. We had enough of sympathy for fifty years; it never brought us anything; and we would rather have an angry man going to the government and saying, my business is interfered with and I won't submit to its being interfered with any longer because you won't give women the vote, than to have a gentleman come onto our platforms year in and year out and talk about his ardent sympathy with woman suffrage.

"Put them in prison," they said; "that will stop it." But

it didn't stop it. They put women in prison for long terms of imprisonment, for making a nuisance of themselves—that was the expression when they took petitions in their hands to the door of the House of Commons; and they thought that by sending them to prison, giving them a day's imprisonment, would cause them to all settle down again and there would be no further trouble. But it didn't happen so at all: instead of the women giving it up, more women did it, and more and more and more women did it until there were three hundred women at a time, who had not broken a single law, only "made a nuisance of themselves" as the politicians say.

The whole argument with the anti-suffragists, or even the critical suffragist man, is this: that you can govern human beings without their consent. They have said to us, "Government rests upon force; the women haven't force, so they must submit." Well, we are showing them that government does not rest upon force at all; it rests upon consent. As long as women consent to be unjustly governed, they can be; but directly women say: "We withhold our consent, we will not be governed any longer so long as that government is unjust," not by the forces of civil war can you govern the very weakest woman. You can kill that woman, but she escapes you then; you cannot govern her. And that is, I think, a most valuable demonstration we have been making to the world.

Death or the Vote

Now, I want to say to you who think women cannot succeed, we have brought the government of England to this position, that it has to face this alternative; either women are to be killed or women are to have the vote. I ask American men in this meeting, what would you say if in your State you were faced with that alternative, that you must either kill them or give them their citizenship—women, many of whom you respect, women whom you know have lived useful lives, women whom you know, even if you do not know them personally, are animated with the highest motives, women who are in pursuit of liberty and the power to do useful public service? Well, there is only one answer to that alternative; there is only one way out of it, unless you are prepared to put back

American men to believe in the fundamental principles of democracy, and I never quite feel as if it was a fair field to argue this question with men, because in doing it you have to assume that a man who professes to believe in a Republican form of government does not believe in a Republican form of government, for the only thing that woman's enfranchisement means at all is that a government which claims to be a Republic should be a Republic, and not an aristocracy.

The difficulty with discussing this question with those who oppose us is that they make any number of arguments but none of them have anything to do with the subject. I have never heard an argument against Woman's Suffrage which had anything to do with Woman's Suffrage; they always have something to do with something else, therefore the arguments which we have to make rarely ever have anything to do with the subject, because we have to answer our opponents who always escape the subject as far as possible in order to have any sort of reason in connection with what they say.

Now one of two things is true: either a Republic is a desirable form of government, or else it is not. If it is, then we should have it, if it is not then we ought not to pretend that we have it. We ought, at least, to be true to our ideals, and the men of New York have, for the first time in their lives the rare opportunity, on the second day of next November, of making this state truly a part of a Republic. It is the greatest opportunity which has ever come to the men of the state. They have never had so serious a problem to solve before, they will never have a more serious problem to solve in any future year of our Nation's life, and the thing that disturbs me more than anything else in connection with it is that so few people realize what a profound problem they have to solve on November 2. It is not merely a trifling matter; it is not a little thing that does not concern the state, it is the most vital problem that we could have, and any man who goes to the polls on the second day of next November without thoroughly informing himself in regard to this subject is unworthy to be a citizen of this state, and unfit to cast a ballot.

If Woman's Suffrage is wrong, it is a great wrong; if it is right, it is a profound and fundamental principle, and we all know, if we know what a Republic is, that it is the fundamental principle upon which a Republic must rise. Let us see where we are as a people; how we act here and what we think we are. The difficulty with the men of this country is that they are so consistent in their inconsistency that they are not aware of having been inconsistent; because their consistency has been so continuous and their inconsistency so consecutive that it has never been broken, from the beginning of our Nation's life to the present time. If we trace our history back we will find that from the very dawn of our existence as a people, men have been imbued with a spirit and a vision more lofty than they have been able to live; they have been led by visions of the sublimest truth, both in regard to religion and in regard to government that ever inspired the souls of men from the time the Puritans left the old world to come to this country, led by the Divine ideal which is the sublimest and supremest ideal in religious freedom which men have ever known, the theory that a man has a right to worship God according to the dictates of his own conscience, without the intervention of any other man or any other group of men. And it was this theory, this vision of the right of the human soul which led men first to the shores of this country. . . .

"It Is Not Good for Man to Stand Alone"

God said in the beginning "It is not good for man to stand alone" [Gen. 2:18].[1] That is why we are here tonight, and that is all that woman's suffrage means; just to repeat again and again that first declaration of the Divine, "It is not good for man to stand alone," and so the women of this state are asking that the word "male" shall be stricken out of the Constitution altogether and that the Constitution stand as it ought to have stood in the beginning and as it must before this state is any part of a Republic. Every citizen possessing the necessary qualifications shall be entitled to cast one vote at every election, and have that vote counted. We are not asking, as our anti-suffrage friends think we are, for any of the awful things that we hear will happen if we are allowed to

---

1. The actual words are "And the Lord God said, It is not good that the man should be alone; I will make him an help meet for him."

vote; we are simply asking that that government which professes to be a Republic shall be a Republic and not pretend to be what it is not.

Now what is a Republic? Take your dictionary, encyclopedia, lexicon or anything else you like and look up the definition and you will find that a Republic is a form of government in which the laws are enacted by representatives elected by the people. Now when did the people of New York ever elect their representatives? Never in the world. The men of New York have, and I grant you that men are people, admirable people, as far as they go, but they only go half way. There is still another half of the people who have not elected representatives, and you never read a definition of a Republic in which half of the people elect representatives to govern the whole of the people. That is an aristocracy and that is just what we are. We have been many kinds of aristocracies. We have been a hierarchy of church members, then an aristocracy of wealth, then an oligarchy of sex.

There are two old theories which are dying today. Dying hard but dying. One of them is dying on the plains of Flanders and the mountains of Galicia and Austria and that is the theory of the divine right of kings. The other is dying here in the state of New York and Massachusetts and New Jersey and Pennsylvania and that is the divine right of sex. Neither of them had a foundation in reason, or justice or common sense.

Now I want to make this proposition and I believe every man will accept it. Of course he will if he is intelligent. Whenever a Republic prescribes the qualifications as applies equally to all the citizens of the Republic, so that when the Republic says in order to vote, a citizen must be twenty-one years of age, it applies to all alike, there is no discrimination against any race or sex. When the government says that a citizen must be a native born citizen or a naturalized citizen, that applies to all; we are either born or naturalized, somehow or other we are here. Whenever the government says that a citizen, in order to vote, must be a resident of a community a certain length of time, and of the state a certain length of time, and of the nation a certain length of time, that applies to all equally. There is no discrimination.

We might go further and we might say that in order to

vote the citizen must be able to read his ballot. We have not gone that far yet. We have been very careful of male ignorance in these United States. I was much interested, as perhaps many of you, in reading the Congressional Record this last winter over the debate over the immigration bill, and when that illiteracy clause was introduced into the immigration bill, what fear there was in the souls of men for fear we would do injustice to some of the people who might want to come to our shores, and I was much interested in the language in which the President [Woodrow Wilson] vetoed the bill, when he declared that by inserting the clause we would keep out of our shores a large body of very excellent people. I could not help wondering then how it happens that male ignorance is so much less ignorant than female ignorance. When I hear people say that if women were permitted to vote a large body of ignorant people would vote, and therefore because an ignorant woman would vote, no intelligent women should be allowed to vote. I wonder why we have made it so easy for male ignorance and so hard for female ignorance.

When I was a girl, years ago, I lived in the back woods, and there the number of votes cast at each election depended entirely upon the size of the ballot box. We had what was known as the old tissue ballots and the man who got the most tissue in was the man elected. Now the best part of our community was very much disturbed by this method, and they did not know what to do in order to get a ballot both safe and secret; but they heard that over in Australia, where the women voted, they had a ballot which was both safe and secret, so we went over there and we got the Australian ballot and brought it there [sic]. But when we got it over we found it was not adapted to this country, because in Australia they have to be able to read their ballot. Now the question was how could we adapt it to our conditions? Someone discovered that if you should put a symbol at the head of each column, like a rooster, or an eagle, or a hand holding a hammer, that if a man has intelligence to know the difference between a rooster and an eagle he will know which political party to vote for, and when the ballot was adapted it was a very beautiful ballot, it looked like a page from *Life*.

Now almost any American woman could vote that ballot,

or if she had not that intelligence to know the difference between an eagle and a rooster, we could take the eagle out and put in the hen. Now when we take so much pains to adapt the ballot to the male intelligence of the United States, we should be very humble when we talk about female ignorance. Now if we should take a vote and the men had to read their ballot in order to vote it, more women could vote than men.

An Insurmountable Barrier

But when the government says not only that you must be twenty-one years of age, a resident of the community and a native born or naturalized, those are qualifications, but when it says that an elector must be a male, that is not a qualification for citizenship; that is an insurmountable barrier between half of the people and the other half, and no government which erects an insurmountable barrier between one half of the citizens and their rights as citizens can call itself a Republic. It is only an aristocracy. That barrier must be removed before that government can become a Republic, and that is exactly what we are asking now, that the last step in this evolutionary process shall be taken on November 2d, and that this great state of New York shall become in fact, as it is in theory, a part of a government of the people, by the people and for the people.

Men know the inconsistencies themselves; they realize it in one way while they do not realize it in another, because you never heard a man make a political speech when he did not speak of this country as a whole as though the thing existed which does not exist and that is that the people were equally free, because you hear them declare over and over again on the Fourth of July "Under God, the people rule." They know it is not true but they say it with a great hurrah, and then they repeat over and over again that clause from the Declaration of Independence, "Governments derive their just powers from the consent of the governed," and then they see how they can prevent half of us from giving our consent to anything, and then they give it to us on the Fourth of July in two languages, so if [it] is not true in one it will be in the other, "vox populi, vox Dei." "The voice of the people is the voice of God," and the orator forgets that in the people's voice there is a soprano as well as a bass. If the voice of the people is the voice of God, how are we ever going to know what God's voice is when we are content to listen to a bass solo? Now if it is true that the voice of the people is the voice of God, we will never know what the Deity's voice in government is until the bass and soprano are mingled together, the result of which will be a divine harmony. Take any of the magnificent appeals for freedom which men make, and rob them of their universal application and you take the very life and soul out of them.

Where is the difficulty? Just in one thing and one thing only, that men are so sentimental. We used to believe that women were the sentimental sex, but they cannot hold a tallow candle compared with the arc light of the men. Men are so sentimental in their attitude about women that they cannot reason about them. Now men are usually very fair to each other. I think the average man recognizes that he has no more right to anything at the hands of the government than has every other man. He has no right at all to anything which every other man has not an equal right with himself. He says why have I a right to certain things in the government; why have I a right to life and liberty; why have I a right to this or this? Does he say because I am a man? Not at all, because I am human, and being human I have a right to everything which belongs to humanity, and every right which any other human being has, I have. And then he says of his neighbor, and my neighbor he also is human, therefore every right which belongs to me as a human being, belongs to him as a human being, and I have no right to anything under the government to which he is not equally entitled.

And then up comes a woman, and then they say now she's a woman; she is not quite human, but she is my wife, or my sister, or my daughter, or an aunt, or my cousin. She is not quite human, she is only related to a human, and being related to a human, a human will take care of her. So we have had that care-taking human being to look after us, and they have not recognized that women too are equally human with men. Now if men could forget for a minute—I believe the anti-suffragists say that we want men to forget that we are related to them, they don't know me—if for a minute they could forget our relationship and remember that we are equally human with themselves, then they would say—yes, and this human being, not because she is a woman, but because she is human is entitled to every privilege and every right under the government which I, as a human being am entitled to. The only reason why men do not see as fairly in regard to women as they do in regard to each other is because they have looked upon us from an altogether different plane than what they have looked at men; that is because women have been the homemakers while men have been the so-called protectors, in the period of the world's civilization when people needed to be protected. I know that they say that men protect us now and when we ask them what they are protecting us from, the only answer they can give is from themselves. I do not think that men need any very great credit for protecting us from themselves. They are not protecting us from any special thing from which we could not protect ourselves except themselves. Now this old-time idea of protection was all right when the world needed this protection, but today the protection in civilization comes from within and not from without.

What are the arguments which our good Anti friends give us? We know that lately they have stopped to argue and call suffragist all sorts of creatures. If there is anything we believe that we do not believe, we have not heard about them, so the cry goes out of this; the cry of the infant's mind; the cry of a little child. The anti-suffragists' cries are all the cries of little children who are afraid of the unborn and are forever crying, "The goblins will catch you if you don't watch out." So that anything that has not been should not be and all that is is right, when as a matter of fact if the world believed that, we would be in a statical [sic] condition and never move, except back like a crab. And so the cries go on.

When suffragists are feminists, and when I ask what that is, no one is able to tell me. I would give anything to know what a feminist is. They say, would you like to be a feminist? If I could find out I would, you either have to be masculine or feminine and I prefer feminine. Then they cry that we are socialists, and anarchists. Just how a human can be both at the same time, I really do not know. If I know what socialism means it means absolute government and anarchism means no government at all. So we are feminists, socialists, anarchists and mormons or spinsters. Now that is about the list. I have not heard the last speech. Now as a matter of fact, as a unit we are nothing, as individuals we are like all other individuals.

A Person's Right to Have Voice in Government

We have our theories, our beliefs, but as suffragists we have but one belief, but one principle, but one theory and that is the right of a human being to have a voice in the government under which he or she lives, on that we agree, if on nothing else. Whether we agree or not on religion or politics we are not concerned. A clergyman asked me the other day, "By the way, what church does your official board belong to?" I said I don't know. He said, "Don't you know what religion your official board believes?" I said, "Really it never occurred to me, but I will hunt them up and see, they are not elected to my board because they believe in any particular church." We had no concern either as to what we believe as religionists or as to what we believe as women in regard to theories of government, except that one fundamental theory in the right of democracy. We do not believe in this fad or the other, but whenever any question is to be settled in any community, then the people of that community shall settle that question, the women people equally with the men people. That is all there is to it, and yet when it comes to arguing our case they bring up all sorts of arguments, and the beauty of it is they always answer all their own arguments. They never make an argument but they answer it. When I was asked to answer one of their debates I said, "What is the use? Divide up their literature and let them destroy themselves."

I was followed up last year by a young married woman from New Jersey. She left her husband and home for three months to tell the women that their place was at home, and that they could not leave home long enough to go to the ballot box, and she brought all her arguments out in pairs and backed them up by statistics. The anti-suffragist can gather more statistics than any other person I ever saw, and there is nothing so sweet and calm as when they say, "You cannot deny this, because here are the figures, and figures never lie." Well they don't, but some liars figure.

When they start out they always begin the same. She started by proving that it was no use to give the women the ballot because if they did have it they would not use it, and she had statistics to prove it. If we would not use it, then I really cannot see the harm of giving it to us, we would not hurt anybody with it and what an easy way for you men to get rid of us. No more suffrage meetings, never any nagging you again, no one could blame you for anything that went wrong with the town, if it did not run right, all you would have to say is, you have the power, why don't you go ahead and clean up.

Then the young lady, unfortunately for her first argument, proved by statistics, of which she had many, the awful results which happened where women did have the ballot; what awful laws have been brought about by women's vote; the conditions that prevail in the homes and how deeply women get interested in politics, because women are hysterical, and we cannot think of anything else, we just forget our families, cease to care for our children, cease to love our husbands and just go to the polls and vote and keep on voting for ten hours a day 365 days in the year, never let up, if we ever get to the polls once you will never get us home, so that the women will not vote at all, and they will not do anything but vote. Now these are two very strong anti-suffrage arguments and they can prove them by figures.

Then they will tell you that if women are permitted to vote it will be a great expense and no use because wives will vote just as their husbands do; even if we have no husbands, that would not affect the result because we would vote just as our husbands would vote if we had one. How I wish the anti-suffragists could make the men believe that; if they could make men believe that the women would vote just as they wanted them to, do you think we would ever have to make another speech or hold another meeting, we would have to vote whether we wanted to or not.

And then the very one who will tell you that women will vote just as their husbands do will tell you in five minutes that they will not vote as their husbands will and then the discord in the homes, and the divorce. Why, they have discovered that in Colorado there are more divorces than there were before women began to vote, but they have forgotten to tell you that there are four times as many people in Colorado today as there were when women began to vote, and that may have some effect, particularly as these people went from the East.

Then they will tell you all the trouble that happens in the home. A gentleman told me that in California—and when he was talking I had a wonderful thing pass through my mind, because he said he and his wife had lived together for twenty years and never had a difference in opinion in the whole twenty years and he was afraid if women began to vote that his wife would vote differently from him and then that beautiful harmony which they had had for twenty years would be broken, and all the time he was talking I could not help wondering which was the idiot—because I knew that no intelligent human beings could live together for twenty years and not have differences of opinion. All the time he was talking I looked at that splendid type of manhood and thought, how would a man feel being tagged up by a little woman for twenty years saying "me too, me too." I would not want to live in a house with a human being for twenty hours who agreed with everything I said. The stagnation of a frog pond would be hilarious compared to that. What a reflection is that on men. If we should say that about men we would never hear the last of it. Now it may be that the kind of men being [sic] that the anti-suffragists live with is that kind, but they are not the kind we live with and we could not do it. Great big overgrown babies! Cannot be disputed without having a row! While we do not believe that men are saints, by any means, we do believe that the average American man is a fairly good sort of a fellow. . . .

Then the people will tell you that women are so burdened with their duties that they cannot vote, and then they will tell you that women are the leisure class and the men are worked to death; but the funniest argument of the lady who followed me about in the West: Out there they were great on the temperance question, and she declared that we were not prohibition, or she declared that we were. Now in North Dakota, which is one of the first prohibition states, and they are dry because they want to be dry. In that state she wanted to prove to them that if women were allowed to vote they would vote North Dakota wet and she had her figures; that women had not voted San Francisco dry, or Portland dry or Chicago dry. Of course we had not voted on the question in Chicago, but that did not matter. Then we went to Montana, which is wet. They have it wet there because they want it wet, so that any argument that she could bring to bear upon them to prove that we would make North Dakota wet and keep it wet would have given us the state, but that would not work, so she brought out the figures out of her pocket to prove to the men of Montana that if women were allowed to vote in Montana they would vote Montana dry. She proved that in two years in Illinois they had voted ninety-six towns dry, and that at that rate we would soon get over Montana and have it dry. Then I went to Nebraska and as soon as I reached there a reporter came and asked me the question "How are the women going to vote on the prohibition question?" I said "I really don't know. I know how we will vote in North Dakota, we will vote dry [sic] in North Dakota; in Montana we will vote dry, but how we will vote in Nebraska, I don't know, but I will let you know just as soon as the lady from New Jersey comes."

We will either vote as our husbands vote or we will not vote as our husbands vote. We either have time to vote or we don't have time to vote. We will either not vote at all or we will vote all the time. It reminds me of the story of the old Irish woman who had twin boys and they were so much alike that the neighbors could not tell them apart, and the mother always seemed to be able to tell them apart, so one of the neighbors said, "Now Mrs. Mahoney, you have two of the finest twin boys I ever saw in all my life, but how do you know them apart." "Oh," she says, "That's easy enough, anyone could tell them apart. When I want to know which is which I just put my finger in Patsey's mouth and if he bites it is Mikey."

The Fundamental Question of Democracy

Now what does it matter whether the women will vote as their husbands do or will not vote; whether they have time or have not; or whether they will vote for prohibition or not. What has that to do with the fundamental question of democracy, no one has yet discovered. But they cannot argue on that; they cannot argue on the fundamental basis of our existence so that they have to get off on all these side tracks to get anything approaching argument. So they tell you that democracy is a form of government. It is not. It was before governments were; it will prevail when governments cease to be; it is more than a form of government; it is a great spiritual force emanating from the heart of the Infinite, transforming human character until some day, some day in the distant future, man by the power of the spirit of democracy, will be able to look back into the face of the Infinite and answer, as man cannot answer today, "One is our Father, even God, and all we people are the children of one family." And when democracy has taken possession of human lives no man will ask for himself any thing which he is not willing to grant to his neighbor, whether that neighbor be a man or a woman; no man will then be willing to allow another man to rise to power on his shoulders, nor will he be willing to rise to power on the shoulders of another prostrate human being. But that has not yet taken possession of us, but some day we will be free, and we are getting nearer and nearer to it all the time; and never in this history of our country had the men and women of this nation a better right to approach it than they have today; never in the history of the nation did it stand out so splendidly as it stands today, and never ought we men and women to be more grateful for anything than that there presides in the White House today a man of peace.

And so our good friends go on with one thing after another and they say if women should vote they will have to sit on the jury and they ask whether we will like to see a woman sitting on a jury. I have seen some juries that ought to be sat on, and I have seen some women that would be glad to sit on anything. When a woman stands up all day behind a counter, or when she stands all day doing a washing, she is glad enough to sit; and when she stands for seventy-five cents, she would like to sit for two dollars a day. But don't you think we need some women on juries in this country? You read your paper and you read that one day last week or the week before or the week before a little girl went out to school and never came back; another little girl was sent on an errand and never came back; another little girl was left in charge of a little sister and her mother went out to work and when she returned the little girl was not there, and you read it over and over again, and the horror of it strikes you. You read that in these United States five thousand young girls go out and never come back, don't you think that the men and women, the vampires of our country who fatten and grow rich on the ignorance and innocence of children would rather face Satan himself than a jury of mothers? I would like to see some juries of mothers. I lived in the slums of Boston for three years and I know the need of juries of mothers.

Then they tell us that if women were permitted to vote that they would take office, and you would suppose that we just took office in this country. There is a difference of getting an office in this country and in Europe. In England a man stands for Parliament and in this country he runs for Congress, and so long as it is a question of running for office I don't think women have much chance, especially with our present hobbles.[2]

There are some women who want to hold office and I may as well own up, I am one of them. I have been wanting to hold office for more than thirty-five years. Thirty-five years ago I lived in the slums of Boston and ever since then I have wanted to hold office. I have applied to the mayor to be made an officer; I wanted to be the greatest office holder in the world, I wanted the position of the man I think is to be the most envied, as far as ability to do good is concerned, and that is a policeman [sic]. I have always wanted to be a policeman and I have applied to be appointed policeman and the very first question that was asked me was, "Could you knock a man down and take him to jail?" That is some people's idea of the highest service that a policeman can render a community. Knock somebody down and take him to jail. My idea is not so much to arrest criminals as it is to prevent crime. That is what is needed in the police force of every community. When I lived for three years in the back alleys of

2. A hobble skirt was a long skirt, popular between 1910 and 1914, that was so narrow below the knees that it prevented a normal stride.

Boston, I saw there that it was needed to prevent crime and from that day to this I believe there is no great public gathering of any sort whatever where we do not need women on the police force; we need them at every moving picture show, every dance house, every restaurant, every hotel, and every great store with a great bargain counter and every park and every resort where the vampires who fatten on the crimes and vices of men and women gather. We need women on the police force and we will have them there some day.

If women vote will they go to war? They are great on having us fight. They tell you that the government rests on force, but there are a great many kinds of force in this world, and never in the history of man were the words of the Scriptures proved to the extent that they are today, that the men of the nation that lives by the sword shall die by the sword. When I was speaking in North Dakota from an automobile with a great crowd and a great number of men gathered around a man who had been sitting in front of a store whittling a stick called out to another man and asked if women get the vote will they go over to Germany and fight the Germans? I said, "Why no, why should we go over to Germany and fight Germans?" I said, why no, why over here to fight [sic], if German men come over here would you fight?" I said, "Why should we women fight men, but if Germany should send an army of women over here, then we would show you what we would do. We would go down and meet them and say, 'Come on, let's go up to the opera house and talk this matter over.' It might grow wearisome but it would not be death.". . .

No, we women do not want the ballot in order that we may fight, but we do want the ballot in order that we may help men to keep from fighting, whether it is in war or in peace; whether it is in the home or in the state, just as the home is not without the man, so the state is not without the woman, and you can no more build up homes without men than you can build up the state without women. We are needed everywhere where human life is. We are needed everywhere where human problems are to [be] solve[d] and men and women must go through this world together from the cradle to the grave, it is God's way and it is the fundamental principle of a Republican form of government.

A Woman's Civil Right

Betty Friedan

During the late 1950s, Betty Friedan, a college-educated housewife and mother, began to document the discontent of suburban housewives—a discontent that she described as "the problem that has no name." In 1963, Friedan published her findings in *The Feminine Mystique*, which rapidly became an international best-seller and served as a catalyst for the women's liberation movement.

The National Organization for Women (NOW), founded by Friedan in 1966, became the first organization to articulate the women's liberation movement's main goals: to bring women into full participation in the mainstream of American society; to eradicate discrimination against women in the workplace, politics, and law; and to challenge the traditional roles of men as breadwinners and women as homemakers.

The right to an abortion was another key issue for women's liberationists, who felt that women did not have equal status in society if they could not control their reproductive choices. At a 1969 national conference for the repeal of laws prohibiting abortion, Friedan argues that motherhood will become a positive act only when women are accorded the freedom to decide when and if they become mothers.

Women, even though they're almost too visible as sex objects in this country, are invisible people. As the Negro was the invisible man, so women are the invisible people in America today: women who have a share in the decisions of the mainstream of government, of politics, of the church—who don't just cook the church supper, but preach the sermon; who don't just look up the ZIP codes and address the envelopes, but make the political decisions; who don't just do the housework of industry, but make some of the executive decisions. Women, above all, who say what their own lives and personalities are going to be, and no longer listen to or even permit male experts to define what 'feminine' is or isn't.

Women's Liberation

The essence of the denigration of women is our definition as sex object. To confront our inequality, therefore, we must confront both society's denigration of us in these terms and our own self-denigration as people.

Am I saying that women must be liberated from sex? No. I am saying that sex will only be liberated to be a human dialogue, sex will only cease to be a sniggering, dirty joke and an obsession in this society, when women become active self-determining people, liberated to a creativity beyond motherhood, to a full human creativity.

Am I saying that women must be liberated from motherhood? No. I am saying that motherhood will only be a joyous and responsible human act when women are free to make, with full conscious choice and full human responsibility, the decisions to become mothers. Then, and only then, will they be able to embrace motherhood without conflict, when they will be able to define themselves not just as somebody's mother, not just as servants of children, not just as breeding receptacles, but as people for whom motherhood is a freely chosen part of life, freely celebrated while it lasts, but for whom creativity has many more dimensions, as it has for men.

Then, and only then, will motherhood cease to be a curse and a chain for men and for children. For despite all the lip service paid to motherhood today, all the roses sent on Mother's Day, all the commercials and the hypocritical ladies' magazines' celebration of women in their roles as housewives and mothers, the fact is that all television or night-club comics have to do is go before a microphone and say the words 'my wife,' and the whole audience erupts into gales of guilty, vicious and obscene laughter.

The hostility between the sexes has never been worse. The image of women in avant-garde plays, novels and movies, and behind the family situation comedies on television is that mothers are man-devouring, cannibalistic monsters, or else Lolitas, sex objects—and objects not even of heterosexual impulse, but of sadomasochism. That impulse—the punishment of women—is much more of a factor in the abortion question than anybody ever admits.

Motherhood is a bane almost by definition, or at least partly so, as long as women are forced to be mothers—and only mothers—against their will. Like a cancer cell living its life through another cell, women today are forced to live too much through their children and husbands (they are too dependent on them, and therefore are forced to take too much varied resentment, vindictiveness, inexpressible resentment and rage out on their husbands and children).

Perhaps it is the least understood fact of American political life: the enormous buried violence of women in this country today. Like all oppressed people, women have been taking their violence out on their own bodies, in all the maladies with which they plague the MDs and the psychoanalysts. Inadvertently, and in subtle and insidious ways, they have been taking their violence out, too, on their children and on their husbands, and sometimes they're not so subtle.

The battered-child syndrome that we are hearing more and more about from our hospitals is almost always to be found in the instance of unwanted children, and women are doing the battering, as much or more than men. In the case histories of psychologically and physically maimed children, the woman is always the villain, and the reason is our definition of her: not only as passive sex object, but as mother, servant, someone else's mother, someone else's wife.

Am I saying that women have to be liberated from men? That men are the enemy? No. I am saying the *men* will only be truly liberated to love women and to be fully themselves when women are liberated to have a full say in the decisions of their lives and their society.

Until that happens, men are going to bear the guilty burden of the passive destiny they have forced upon women, the suppressed resentment, the sterility of love when it is not between two fully active, joyous people, but has in it the element of exploitation. And men will not be free to be all they can be as long as they must live up to an image of masculinity that disallows all the tenderness and sensitivity in a man, all that might be considered feminine. Men have enormous capacities in them that they have to repress and fear in order to live up to the obsolete, brutal, bear-killing, Ernest Hemingway, crew-cut Prussian, napalm-all-the-children-in-Vietnam, bang-bang-you're-dead image of masculinity. Men are not allowed to admit that they sometimes are afraid. They are not allowed to express their own sensitivity, their own need to be passive sometimes and not always active. Men are not allowed to cry. So they are only half-human, as women are only half-human, until we can go this next step forward. All the burdens and responsibilities that men are supposed to shoulder alone makes them, I think, resent women's pedestal, much as that pedestal may be a burden for women.

The Real Sexual Revolution

This is the real sexual revolution. Not the cheap headlines in the papers about at what age boys and girls go to bed with each other and whether they do it with or without the benefit of marriage. That's the least of it. The real sexual revolution is the emergence of women from passivity, from the point where they are the easiest victims for all the seductions, the waste, the worshiping of false gods in our affluent society, to full self-determination and full dignity. And it is the emergence of men from the stage where they are inadvertent brutes and masters to sensitive, complete humanity.

This revolution cannot happen without radical changes in the family as we know it today; in our concepts of marriage and love, in our architecture, our cities, our theology, our politics, our art. Not that women are special. Not that women are superior. But these expressions of human creativity are bound to be infinitely more various and enriching when women and men are allowed to relate to each other beyond the strict confines of the *Ladies' Home Journal*'s definition of the Mamma and Papa marriage.

If we are finally allowed to become full people, not only will children be born and brought up with more love and responsibility than today, but we will break out of the confines of that sterile little suburban family to relate to each other in terms of all of the possible dimensions of our personalities— male and female, as comrades, as colleagues, as friends, as lovers. And without so much hate and jealousy and buried resentment and hypocrisies, there will be a whole new sense of love that will make what we call love on Valentine's Day look very pallid.

It's crucial, therefore, that we see this question of abortion as more than a quantitative move, more than a politically expedient move. Abortion repeal is not a question of political expediency. It is part of something greater. It is historic that we are addressing ourselves this weekend to perhaps the first national confrontation of women and men. Women's voices are finally being heard aloud, saying it the way it is about the question of abortion both in its most basic sense of morality and in its new political sense as part of the unfinished revolution of sexual equality.

In this confrontation, we are making an important milestone in this marvelous revolution that began long before any of us here were born and which still has a long way to go. As the pioneers from Mary Wollstonecraft[1] to Margaret Sanger[2] gave us the consciousness that brought us from our several directions here, so we here, in changing the very terms of the debate on abortion to assert woman's right to choose, and to define the terms of our lives ourselves, move women further to full human dignity. Today, we moved history forward.

1. British author of the first great feminist treatise, *A Vindication of the Rights of Woman* (1792). 2. Opened the country's first birth control clinic in 1916, despite the fact that contraception was illegal. Later founded Planned Parenthood.

Funeral Oration for the Burial of Traditional Womanhood

Kathie Amatniek

Dissatisfied with the relatively conservative approach of organizations such as NOW, so-called radical feminists united to voice their anger at women's societal role as sexual objects for men. Radical feminists spoke critically of marriage and motherhood; many advocated lesbianism. Their controversial tactics, which included dramatic staged events, drew considerable media attention.

One of the most provocative events of this kind occurred on January 15, 1968, at the nation's capital. During a protest of the Vietnam War, thousands of women broke off from the march to attend a mock funeral for "the burial of traditional womanhood." The crowd held aloft an enormous dummy of a quintessentially feminine woman adorned with blonde curls and garters.

Kathie Amatniek, an organizer of the effort, delivered a speech entitled, "Funeral Oration for the Burial of Traditional Womanhood," in which she urges women to recognize the ways that traditional roles deprive women of their humanity. Amatniek argues that women must reject their status as submissive beings if they are to be effective demonstrators against the war.

From Kathie Amatniek, "Funeral Oration for the Burial of Traditional Womanhood," speech delivered at the U.S. Capitol, Washington, D.C., January 15, 1968. Reprinted by arrangement with the Rare Book, Manuscript, and Special Collections Library, Duke University, Durham, North Carolina.

You see here the remains of a female human being who during her all too short a lifetime was a familiar figure to billions of people in every corner of the world. Although scientists would classify this specimen within the genus species of homo sapiens, for many years there has been considerable controversy as to whether she really belonged in some kind of *sub*-species of the genus. While the human being was distinguished as an animal who freed himself from his biological limitations by developing technology and expanding his consciousness, traditional Womanhood has been recognized, defined and valued for her biological characteristics only and those social functions closely related to her biological characteristics.

As human beings, both men and women were sexual creatures and they shared their sexuality. But the other areas of humanity were closed off to Traditional Womanhood . . . the areas which, as has already been noted, were more characteristically human, less limited by biology. For some reason, man said to woman: you are less sexual when you participate in those other things, you are no longer attractive to me if you do so. I like you quiet and submissive. It makes me feel as if you don't love me, if you fail to let me do all the talking . . . if you actually have something to say yourself. Or else, when I like you to be charming and well-educated . . . entertainment for me and an intelligent mother for my children . . . these qualities are for me and for me alone. When you confront the world outside the home—the world where I operate as an individual self as well as a husband and father—then, for some reason, I feel you are a challenge to me and you become sexless and aggressive.

If you turn me off too much, you know, I'll find myself another woman. And if that happens, what will you do? You'll be a nobody, that's what you'll be. An old maid, if I haven't deigned to marry you yet. A divorced woman . . . with some children, no doubt. Without me, you won't even have your sexuality anymore, that little bit of humanity which I have allowed you. And even if you manage to solve that problem in some kind of perverse way, it's going to be hard for you.

What kinds of jobs can you get to keep yourself in comfort? I control those few interesting, challenging ones. And I control the salaries on all the other kinds of jobs from which my fellow men who work at them will at least get the satisfaction of more *pay* than you. And I control the government and its money which, you can bet your tax dollar, isn't going to get allotted for enough good nursery schools to put your children into so you can go out to work. And because of all these things, there can always be another woman in my life, when you no longer *serve* my needs.

And so Traditional Womanhood, even if she was unhappy with her lot, believed that there was nothing she could do about it. She blamed herself for her limitations and she tried to *adapt*. She told herself and she told others that she was happy as half a person, as the "better half" of someone else, as the mother of others, powerless in her own right.

Traditional Womanhood Died Today

Though Traditional Womanhood was a hardy dame, the grand old lady finally died today—her doctor said, of a bad case of shock. Her flattering menfolk had managed to keep her alive for thousands of years. She survived the Amazon challenge. She survived the Lysistrata challenge. She survived the Feminist challenge. And she survived many face-liftings. She was burning her candle at one end on a dull wick and she went out slowly, but she finally went . . . not with a bang but a whimper.

There are some grounds for believing that our march today contributed to the lady's timely demise and this is partly the reason we have decided to hold her funeral here. The old hen, it turns out, was somewhat disturbed to hear *us*—other women, that is—asserting ourselves just this least little bit about critical problems in the world controlled by men. And it was particularly frightening to her to see other women, we women, asserting ourselves together, however precariously, in some kind of solidarity, instead of completely resenting each other, being embarrassed by each other, hating each other and hating ourselves.

And we were even attempting to organize ourselves on the basis of power . . . that little bit of power we are told we have here in America . . . the so-called power of wives and mothers. That this power is only a *substitute* for power, that it really amounts to nothing politically, is the reason why all of us attending this funeral must bury Traditional Womanhood tonight. We must bury her in Arlington Cemetery, however crowded it is by now. For in Arlington Cemetery, our national monument to war, alongside Traditional Manhood is her natural resting place.

Now some sisters here are probably wondering why we should bother with such an unimportant matter at a time like this. Why should we bury Traditional Womanhood while hundreds of thousands of human beings are being brutally slaughtered in our names . . . when it would seem that our number one task is to devote our energies directly to ending this slaughter or else solve what seem to be more desperate problems at home?

The Problem of Women in America

Sisters who ask a question like this are failing to see that they really do have a problem as women in America . . . that their problem is social, not merely personal . . . and that their problem is so closely related and interlocked with the other problems in our country, the very problem of war itself . . . that we cannot hope to move toward a better world or even a truly democratic society at home until we begin to solve our own problems.

How many sisters failed to join our march today because they were afraid their husbands would disapprove? How many more sisters failed to join us today because they've been taught to believe that women are silly and a women's march even sillier? And how many millions of sisters all across America failed to join us because they think so little of themselves that they feel incapable of thinking *for* themselves . . . about the war in Vietnam or anything else? And if some sisters come to conclusions of their own, how many others of us fail to express these ideas, much less argue and demonstrate for them, because we're afraid of seeming unattractive, silly, "uppity"? To the America watching us, after all, we here on this march are mere women, looking silly and unattractive.

Yes, sisters, we have a problem as women all right, a problem which renders us powerless and ineffective over the issues of war and peace, as well as over our own lives. And although our problem is Traditional Manhood as much as Traditional Womanhood, we women must begin on the solution.

We must see that we can only solve our problem together, that we cannot solve it individually as earlier Feminist generations attempted to do. We women must organize so that for man there can be no "other woman" when we begin expressing ourselves and acting politically, when we insist to men that they share the housework and child-care, fully and equally, so that we can have independent lives as well.

Human qualities will make us attractive then, not servile qualities. We will want to have daughters as much as we want to have sons. Our children will not become victims of our unconscious resentments and our displaced ambitions. And both our daughters and sons will be free to develop themselves in just the directions they want to go as human beings.

Sisters: men need us, too, after all. And if we just get together and tell our men that we want our freedom as full human beings, that we don't want to live just through our man and his achievements and our mutual offspring, that we want human power in our own right, not just "power behind the throne," that we want neither dominance or submission for anybody, anyplace in Vietnam or in our own homes, and that when we all have our freedom we can truly love each other.

If men fail to see that love, justice and equality are the solution, that domination and exploitation hurt everybody, then our species is truly doomed; for if domination and exploitation and aggression are inherent biological characteristics which cannot be overcome, then nuclear war is inevitable and we will have reached our evolutionary deadend by annihilating ourselves.

And that is why we must bury this lady in Arlington Cemetery tonight, why we must bury Submission alongside Aggression. And that is why we ask you to join us. It is only a symbolic happening, of course, and we have a lot of real work to do. We have new men as well as a new society to build.

A Strategy to Strengthen Women's Political Power

Bella S. Abzug

Bella S. Abzug, a lawyer and U.S. representative who represented Manhattan from 1971 to 1976, gained national notoriety as a vocal advocate for women's rights and an opponent of the Vietnam War. One of the most flamboyant personalities of the women's rights movement, Abzug earned such titles as "Battling Bella," "Hurricane Bella," "Mother Courage," "the Wicked Witch," and "Bellacose Abzug."

In the following speech, delivered to 357 Southern women at the 1972 Southern Women's Conference on Education in Nashville, Abzug reports that women are essentially invisible in the sphere of politics. Arguing that women's equality can never be achieved without equal representation in government, Abzug urges her listeners to organize a unified fight for women's political power.

Roberta Madden, one of the attendants, describes her reaction to Abzug's speech:

> Speaking boldly and confidently, in her husky New York–accented voice, Ms. Abzug acknowledged the "conscious unity" among women everywhere in the country today, a feeling of unity that became almost palpable as she spoke. . . . Looking at her as she stood on the small stage, at the broad-brimmed hat she wears as a trademark, at her strong, sure hands gesturing as she talked, I recognized this solid, sensible, beautifully human woman as *my* representative. "Yes!" I kept thinking all the while, "*that's* what I've been trying to say."

From Bella S. Abzug, "A New Kind of Southern Strategy," speech delivered at the Southern Women's Conference on Education, Nashville, Tennessee, February 12, 1972.

A s cochairwoman of the National Women's Political Caucus, I welcome you to the women's political power movement. . . .

Our women are as diverse as America itself, as diverse as you who have come here today. Women who are young and old, rich and poor, white, black, Chicanas, Puerto Ricans and Indians, women who come from all parties and no parties, women who are in the United States Congress and women who have never held office.

Your presence here indicates the conscious unity that binds you together with thousands of women across the country and the sense of common wrongs and injustices that exists among millions of women, whether they work in universities, factories, offices or in the home.

We are women with many different life styles. Television and the other media which thrive on the offbeat and the sensational have tried to depict the women's liberation movement as an assembly of bra-burning, neurotic, man-hating exhibitionists. Don't let them fool you.

I have been to hundreds of women's meetings and I have yet to see a bra burned.

But I have met and talked to women who were burning with indignation at the wastefulness and stupidity of a society that makes second-class citizens of half its population.

Women, in fact, are 53 percent of the electorate. Yet throughout our history and now, more than a half century after we won the vote, women are still almost invisible in government, in elected posts, in high administrative decision-making positions, in the judiciary.

We are determined to change that. And we intend to do it by organizing ourselves and by reaching out to women everywhere.

I would like to read to you from the Statement of Purpose adopted by the National Women's Political Caucus at its founding meeting. It addressed its appeal to:

> . . . every woman whose abilities have been wasted by the second-class, subservient, underpaid, or powerless positions to which female human beings are consigned
>
> To every woman who sits at home with little control

over her own life, much less the powerful institutions of the country, wondering if there isn't more to life than this

To every woman who must go on welfare because, even when she can get a job, she makes about half the money paid to a man for the same work

To every minority woman who has endured the stigma of being twice-different from the white male ruling class

To every woman who has experienced the ridicule or hostility reserved by this country—and often by its political leaders—for women who dare to express the hopes and ambitions that are natural to every human being

To all these women—and they are nearly all of us—we said that it is time for us to join together to act against the sexism, racism, institutional violence and poverty that disfigure our beautiful land.

We said it is time that women organize to get an equal share of representation and power in the political structures of government.

It is time that we organize to see that women's issues, the priorities of life, not war, are taken seriously and become the policy of government, a government that represents us.

Wherever I go, and I have traveled a great deal in the past year, I have found a strong community of interest among huge numbers of American women, a strong commitment to changing the direction of our society.

Women are in the forefront of the peace movement, the civil rights and equal rights movement, the environment and consumer movements, the child care movement. This is part of your tradition too. It was southern ladies who organized the Committee to Stop Lynching here in the South many years ago, and it was a woman who sat in the *front* of a bus in Montgomery, Alabama, and made history.

Just a few weeks ago I sat in Congress and heard the President[1] give the State of the Union address. There were more than seven hundred of us seated on the main floor of the House. You may have heard the President say, Here we have assembled the Government of the United States, the members of the House, the Senate, the Supreme Court, the Cabinet.

1. Richard M. Nixon, president of the United States during 1969–1974.

I looked around and of these 700 leaders of Government, there were just 12 women. Could anything be more disgraceful? Eleven women out of 435 members of the House. One woman out of 100 in the Senate. No women in the Cabinet. No women on the Supreme Court, although the President has had four separate opportunities to appoint one.

In fact, there were more women up in the balcony than on the floor, and as onlookers their role was to look pretty, to applaud dutifully and to be silent.

The End of Silence

But we have come to the end of silence. There is too much to say. The men haven't done such a great job by themselves. Women look at a nation run by a male executive branch, a male Congress, male governors and legislatures, a male Pentagon, and male corporations and banks, and they rightly ask:

> If we shared equally with men the authority of government, would we condone the spending of more than a trillion dollars in the past twenty-five years for killing and useless weapons—
> - when our cities are dying of neglect
> - when families go hungry in Appalachia
> - when children in South Carolina suffer from malnutrition and are afflicted with worms
> - when people live in shacks or are forced to go on welfare because there are no jobs for them
> - when there are not enough hospitals, doctors and schools
> - when our young people are becoming more and more alienated from a society they regard as without soul or purpose

I think not.

I believe that shutting women out of political power and decision-making roles has resulted in a terrible mutilation of our society. It is at least partly responsible for our present crisis of lopsided priorities and distorted values. It is responsible too for the masculine mystique, the obsession with militarism that has made the nuclear missile the symbol of American power and that equates our national honor with continuing the senseless killing in Indochina, continuing a war which American women—in even larger numbers than men—say must be ended.

As you know, some of the most powerful men in the House are from the South. They hold the leadership posts. They head the most important committees—Armed Services, Appropriations, Ways and Means, and others. They are the ones who decide whether we are to build more bombs or more schools. They are there because of the seniority system and because they are reelected year after year without any significant opposition. Women help elect these men, and then men use their power to deny women their most basic needs.

I hope that this is the year when some of you women will begin to challenge these men and put them on notice that they don't have a lifetime hold on those congressional seats.

Don't get me wrong. I am not saying that the men in Congress are totally indifferent to the needs of women. Many are genuinely concerned. Others are catching on to the fact that they had better be concerned, and still others are now pretending to care.

But it is also a fact of life that it is the victim of discrimination who feels most deeply the injustice of discrimination and who is most determined to end it.

Consider what is happening in Congress in connection with the Equal Employment Opportunity Commission. A filibuster in the Senate has just defeated an attempt to equip the EEOC with effective cease-and-desist power to stop employers from discriminating against women, blacks and other minorities. We lost the same fight in the House, too.

The Facts About Discrimination

The shameful facts of discrimination against black people have been set before the nation, but I wonder how many are fully aware of the scandalous and all-pervasive discrimination against women of all colors.

Do you know that women now make up 37 percent of the labor force . . . that almost thirty million women work, most of them because they need the money . . . that seven out of ten work at menial clerical jobs, and most of the others at service or factory jobs?

Do you know that only 7 percent of doctors are women, earn less than $5,000 a year? Do you know that even when they are better educated than men, they wind up with worse jobs . . . that even when they perform the same work as men, they usually get paid less, and that promotions usually go to men, not women?

Do you know that only 7 percent of doctors are women, and that we have only a toehold in the other professions? Do you know that the number of women in college and university teaching is actually declining?

Do you know about the 4.5 million mothers in the labor force who have youngsters under six? Nearly 6 million preschool children whose mothers have to work to help buy their food and clothing, but in all of this great land we have only enough child care centers to accommodate a half million children. And when we finally passed a child care act at this last session, the President vetoed it. He said it was fiscally irresponsible, and yet a few weeks later he asked for twice as much money—$4 billion—to increase military spending. And he also vetoed it because he said it was a threat to family life!

I would suggest that women are greater authorities on family life than is the President. It is they who bear the children and raise them, many as heads of the family. It is they who work as waitresses, secretaries, hospital aides, factory hands, and in the fields. And it is they who come home and have to clean and cook and care for their children and worry about getting baby sitters when they go to work the next day or night.

If we had more of these real experts in Congress, they would not let the President get away with pious invocations of a nonreal world. They would insist that instead of raising our military budget to $80 billion, as the President proposes, that we allocate money for child care centers, for training programs and more educational opportunities for women, for basic human needs.

And I believe that if we had a truly representative Congress, with at least half of its members women and with much greater representation of blacks and other minorities, we would get real, effective action to end discrimination. We would have not a filibuster, but an EEOC with teeth in it. We would have an Equal Rights Amendment.

I am not elevating women to sainthood, nor am I suggesting that all women share the same views, or that all women are good and all men are bad. But I do believe that because they have been excluded from political power for so long, they see with more clairvoyant eyes the deficiencies of our society. Their work in the voluntary organizations has made them the compassionate defenders of the victims of our distorted priorities. They know intimately the problems of the aged and the sick, of the neglected, miseducated child, the young soldiers returning home wounded in body or spirit.

There are only eleven of us women in the House. Some of us are Democrats, some Republicans, some liberals and some conservatives. But all of us supported the Mansfield Amendment which requires all American troops to be withdrawn from Indochina within six months. I find that very significant and an encouraging omen of things to come.

What is to come? Is this the year when women's political power will come of age? Or are we just going to make noise but no real progress?. . .

Opening Political Institutions to Women

We are prepared to use every means at our disposal to remove the "for men only" sign from American politics and to open wide our political institutions to women and to all underrepresented groups.

We intend to do this not only at the conventions, but in political contests all over the country. We will have more women running this year for local office, for the state legislature, for Congress. Some will run for the experience, and some will run to win. Some are already running. I have been getting phone calls from around the country. A woman is running for governor of Texas. Black women are running for Congress from Texas and California, and there are others who are planning to do so or who have already announced. At some point we're going to get all our women candidates together and introduce them to the nation.

We in the women's political movement have a responsibility to see that we do get some winners and that we pick out contests wisely. I would urge that in every state or region you get together, the sooner the better, and pick your concentration points. Choose your strongest candidates to run against the weakest incumbents. Try to select areas in which you can build coalitions with other underrepresented groups.

Remember, this is the year when the outs—all of us—are demanding "in."

Representatives of young people with a potential strength of twenty-five million new voters met in Chicago recently to organize a Youth Caucus, and they are now setting up caucuses in all the states. The black caucus is well organized, and other minority groups are also joining together to make their political power count.

I believe that with the organization of these groups we have the components of a New Majority—a majority of women, young people, minority groups and other Americans—small businessmen, working people, farmers, poor people—who share in our concerns and needs.

Working together, this New Majority has the capacity to change America, to lead us away from war and to work together instead for a society in which human needs are paramount, in which all people—men and women—who can work will have meaningful employment, in which women will have full citizenship and dignity as individuals, in which our children can learn and live free from the atmosphere of hatred and violence that has despoiled our land for so many years.

These are goals to which I believe most women will respond. What you do here this weekend at this historic first political meeting of southern womanpower will help create that kind of America.

For the Equal Rights Amendment

Shirley Chisholm

In 1968, campaigning under the motto "unbossed and unbought," Shirley Chisholm became the first African-American woman to win a seat in the House of Representatives. Speaking about the publicity she earned upon her election, Chisholm said, "That I am a national figure because I was the first person in 192 years to be at once a congressman, black, and a woman proves, I would think, that our society is not yet either just or free."

One of Chisholm's many goals was to garner congressional support for the Equal Rights Amendment. First drafted by Alice Paul in 1921, the Equal Rights Amendment consisted of three declarations:

Section 1. Equality of rights under the law shall not be denied or abridged by the United States or any state on account of sex.
Section 2. The Congress shall have the power to enforce, by appropriate legislation, the provisions of this article.
Section 3. This amendment shall take effect two years after the date of ratification.

Beginning in 1923, the amendment was introduced in Congress every session. In 1972, it was finally passed; however, it was not ratified by the necessary thirty-eight states by the 1982 deadline. Consequently, the amendment has lost widespread legislative support.

Regarded as one of the most effective orators in Congress, Chisholm was a formidable voice in the quest for the ERA. In "For the Equal Rights Amendment," an ad-

From Shirley Chisholm, speech delivered before the 91st Congress (1970) during hearings on Joint Resolution 264, the Equal Rights Amendment.

dress to the 91st Congress in 1970, Chisholm asserts that
the Equal Rights Amendment would provide a clear legal
basis for the rejection of sex discrimination. She declares
that legal distinctions between the sexes are founded on
archaic views and therefore should be abolished.

M r. Speaker, House Joint Resolution 264, before us
today, which provides for equality under the law
for both men and women, represents one of the
most clear-cut opportunities we are likely to have to declare
our faith in the principles that shaped our Constitution. It
provides a legal basis for attack on the most subtle, most
pervasive and most institutionalized form of prejudice that
exists. Discrimination against women, solely on the basis of
their sex, is so widespread that it seems to many persons normal, natural, and right. Legal expression of prejudice on the
grounds of religious or political belief has become a minor
problem in our society. Prejudice on the basis of race is, at
least, under systematic attack. There is reason for optimism
that it will start to die with the present older generation. It is
time we act to assure full equality of opportunity to those citizens who, although in a majority, suffer the restrictions that
are more commonly imposed on minorities, to women.

The argument that this amendment will not solve the
problem of sex discrimination is not relevant. If the argument
were used against a civil rights bill—as it has been used in the
past—the prejudice that lies behind it would be embarrass-
ing. Of course laws will not eliminate prejudice from the
hearts of human beings. But that is no reason to allow prejudice to continue to be enshrined in our laws—to perpetuate
injustice through inaction.

The amendment is necessary to clarify countless ambigu-
ities and inconsistencies in our legal system. For instance, the
Constitution guarantees due process of law, in the fifth and
fourteenth amendments. But the applicability of due process
to sex distinctions is not clear: Women are excluded from
some State colleges and universities. In some States, restrictions are placed on a married woman who engages in an in-

dependent business. Women may not be chosen for some juries. Women even receive heavier criminal penalties than men who commit the same crime.

What would the legal effects of the equal rights amendment really be? The equal rights amendment would govern only the relationship between the State and its citizens—not relationships between private citizens.

The amendment would be largely self-executing, that is, any Federal or State laws in conflict would be ineffective one year after date of ratification without further action by the Congress or State legislatures.

Opponents of the amendment claim its ratification would throw the law into a state of confusion and would result in much litigation to establish its meaning. This objection overlooks the influence of legislative history in determining intent and the recent activities of many groups preparing for legislative changes in this direction.

State labor laws applying only to women, such as those limiting hours of work and weights to be lifted, would become inoperative unless the legislature amended them to apply to men. As of early 1970 most States would have some laws that would be affected. However, changes are being made so rapidly as a result of Title VII of the Civil Rights Act of 1964, it is likely that by the time the equal rights amendment would become effective, no conflicting State laws would remain.

In any event, there has for years been great controversy as to the usefulness to women of these State labor laws. There has never been any doubt that they worked a hardship on women who need or want to work overtime and on women who need or want better-paying jobs, and there has been no persuasive evidence as to how many women benefit from the archaic policy of the laws. After the Delaware hours law was repealed in 1966, there were no complaints from women to any of the State agencies that might have been approached.

Jury service laws not making women equally liable for jury service would have to be revised.

The selective service law would have to include women, but women would not be required to serve in the Armed Forces where they are not fitted any more than men are required to serve. Military service, while a great responsibility,

is not without benefits, particularly for young men with limited education or training. Since October 1966, 246,000
young men who did not meet the normal mental or physical
requirements have been given opportunities for training and
correcting physical problems. This opportunity is not open to
their sisters. Only girls who have completed high school and
meet high standards on the educational test can volunteer.
Ratification of the amendment would not permit application
of higher standards to women.

Survivorship benefits would be available to husbands of
female workers on the same basis as to wives of male workers. The Social Security Act and the civil service and military
service retirement acts are in conflict.

Public schools and universities could not be limited to
one sex and could not apply different admission standards to
men and women. Laws requiring longer prison sentences for
women than men would be invalid, and equal opportunities
for rehabilitation and vocational training would have to be
provided in public correctional institutions.

Different ages of majority based on sex would have to be
harmonized.

Federal, State, and other governmental bodies would be
obligated to follow nondiscriminatory practices in all aspects
of employment, including public school teachers and State
university and college faculties.

What would be the economic effects of the equal rights
amendment? Direct economic effects would be minor. If any
labor laws applying only to women still remained, their
amendment or repeal would provide opportunity for women
in better-paying jobs in manufacturing. More opportunities
in public vocational and graduate schools for women would
also tend to open up opportunities in better jobs for women.

Indirect effects could be much greater. The focusing of
public attention on the gross legal, economic, and social discrimination against women by hearings and debates in the
Federal and State legislatures would result in changes in attitude of parents, educators, and employers that would bring
about substantial economic changes in the long run.

Sex prejudice cuts both ways. Men are oppressed by the
requirements of the Selective Service Act, by enforced legal

guardianship of minors, and by alimony laws. Each sex, I believe, should be liable when necessary to serve and defend this country.

Each has a responsibility for the support of children.

There are objections raised to wiping out laws protecting women workers. No one would condone exploitation. But what does sex have to do with it? Working conditions and hours that are harmful to women are harmful to men; wages that are unfair for women are unfair for men. Laws setting employment limitations on the basis of sex are irrational, and the proof of this is their inconsistency from State to State. The physical characteristics of men and women are not fixed, but cover two wide spans that have a great deal of overlap. It is obvious, I think, that a robust woman could be more fit for physical labor than a weak man. The choice of occupation would be determined by individual capabilities, and the rewards for equal work should be equal.

This is what it comes down to: artificial distinctions between persons must be wiped out of the law. Legal discrimination between the sexes is, in almost every instance, founded on outmoded views of society and the prescientific beliefs about psychology and physiology. It is time to sweep away these relics of the past and set future generations free of them.

The Need for a Constitutional Amendment

Federal agencies and institutions responsible for the enforcement of equal opportunity laws need the authority of a Constitutional amendment. The 1964 Civil Rights Act and the 1963 Equal Pay Act are not enough; they are limited in their coverage—for instance, one excludes teachers, and the other leaves out administrative and professional women. The Equal Employment Opportunity Commission has not proven to be an adequate device, with its powers limited to investigation, conciliation and recommendation to the Justice Department. In its cases involving sexual discrimination, it has failed in more than one-half. The Justice Department has been even less effective. It has intervened in only one case involving discrimination on the basis of sex, and this was on a procedural point. In a second case, in which both sexual and racial discrimination were alleged, the racial bias charge was given far greater weight.

Evidence of discrimination on the basis of sex should hardly have to be cited here. It is in the Labor Department's employment and salary figures for anyone who is still in doubt. Its elimination will involve so many changes in our State and Federal laws that, without the authority and impetus of this proposed amendment, it will perhaps take another 194 years. We cannot be parties to continuing a delay. The time is clearly now to put this House on record for the fullest expression of that equality of opportunity which our founding fathers professed.

They professed it, but they did not assure it to their daughters, as they tried to do for their sons.

The Constitution they wrote was designed to protect the rights of white, male citizens. As there were no black founding fathers, there were no founding mothers—a great pity, on both counts. It is not too late to complete the work they left undone. Today, here, we should start to do so.

In closing I would like to make one point. Social and psychological effects will be initially more important than legal or economic results. As Leo Kanowitz[1] has pointed out:

> Rules of law that treat of the sexes per se inevitably produce far-reaching effects upon social, psychological and economic aspects of male-female relations beyond the limited confines of legislative chambers and courtrooms. As long as organized legal systems, at once the most respected and most feared of social institutions, continue to differentiate sharply, in treatment or in words, between men and women on the basis of irrelevant anal artificially created distinctions, the likelihood of men and women coming to regard one another primarily as fellow human beings and only secondarily as representatives of another sex will continue to be remote. When men and women are prevented from recognizing one another's essential humanity by sexual prejudices, nourished by legal as well as social institutions, society as a whole remains less than it could otherwise become.

1. Professor of law.

Women's Liberation Is Men's Liberation

Gloria Steinem

The women's liberation movement gained new momentum in the late 1960s with the emergence of charismatic speakers such as Gloria Steinem, a political journalist and a passionate activist for women's rights. Still one of the nation's most famous feminists, Steinem's list of achievements is long: She was an intrepid reporter, the cofounder of *New York Magazine* and the National Women's Political Caucus, a founder and editor of *Ms.* magazine, and the author of several books. Inducted into the Women's Hall of Fame in 1993, Steinem continues to write and speak on the subject of women's rights.

In this excerpt from her commencement address to the 1970 graduating class at Vassar College, Steinem counters beliefs that the women's liberation movement is hostile to men. In truth, she maintains, eliminating traditional gender roles would free both men and women to live life according to their own desires. Later, Steinem stated that the address "was prepared with great misgivings about its reception."

This is the year of Women's Liberation. Or at least, it's the year the press has discovered a movement that has been strong for several years now, and reported it as a small, privileged, rather lunatic event instead of the major revolution in consciousness—in everyone's consciousness, male or female—that I believe it truly is.

From Gloria Steinem, "'Women's Liberation' Aims to Free Men, Too," *The Washington Post*, June 7, 1970. Reprinted by permission of the author.

It is a movement that some call "feminist" but should more accurately be called humanist; a movement that is an integral part of rescuing this country from its old, expensive patterns of elitism, racism and violence.

The first problem for all of us, men and women, is not to learn, but to unlearn. We are filled with the popular wisdom of several centuries just past, and we are terrified to give it up. Patriotism means obedience, age means wisdom, woman means submission, black means inferior: these are preconceptions imbedded so deeply in our thinking that we honestly may not know that they are there.

Unfortunately, authorities who write textbooks are sometimes subject to the same popular wisdom as the rest of us. They gather their proof around it, and end by becoming the theoreticians of the status quo. Using the most respectable of scholarly methods, for instance, English scientists proved definitively that the English were descended from the angels while the Irish were descended from the apes.

It was beautifully done, complete with comparative skull measurements, and it was a rationale for the English domination of the Irish for more than 100 years. I try to remember that when I'm reading Arthur Jensen's current and very impressive work on the limitations of black intelligence, or when I'm reading Lionel Tiger on the inability of women to act in groups.

It wasn't easy for the English to give up their mythic superiority. Indeed, there are quite a few Irish who doubt that they have done it yet. Clearing our minds and government policies of outdated myths is proving to be at least as difficult, but it is also inevitable. Whether it's woman's secondary role in society or the paternalistic role of the United States in the world, the old assumptions just don't work any more.

Part of living this revolution is having the scales fall from our eyes. Every day we see small obvious truths that we had missed before. Our histories, for instance have generally been written for and about white men. Inhabited countries were "discovered" when the first white male set foot there, and most of us learned more about any one European country than we did about Africa and Asia combined.

I confess that, before some consciousness-changing of my own, I would have thought that the women's history courses springing up around the country belonged in the same cultural ghetto as home economics. The truth is that we need Women's Studies almost as much as we need Black Studies, and for exactly the same reason: too many of us have completed a "good" education believing that everything from political power to scientific discovery was the province of white males.

We believed, for instance, that the vote had been "given" to women in some whimsical, benevolent fashion. We never learned about the long desperation of the women's struggle, or about the strength and wisdom of the women who led it. We knew a great deal more about the outdated, male supremacist theories of Sigmund Freud than we did about societies where women had equal responsibility, or even ruled. "Anonymous," Virginia Woolf[1] once said sadly, "was a woman."

A Black Parallel

I don't mean to equate our problems of identity with those that flowed from slavery. But, as Gunnar Myrdal pointed out in his classic study *An American Dilemma,* "In drawing a parallel between the position of, and feeling toward, women and Negroes, we are uncovering a fundamental basis of our culture."

Blacks and women suffer from the same myths of child-like natures; smaller brains; inability to govern themselves, much less white men; limited job skills; identity as sex objects, and so on. Ever since slaves arrived on these shores and were given the legal status of wives—that is, chattel—our legal reforms have followed on each other's heels—with women, I might add, still lagging considerably behind.

President Nixon's Commission on Women concluded that the Supreme Court sanctions discrimination against women—discrimination that it long ago ruled unconstitutional in the case of blacks—but the commission report remains mysteriously unreleased by the White House. An equal rights amendment now up again before the Senate has been delayed by a male-chauvinist Congress for 47 years. Neither blacks nor women have role-models in history: models of individuals who have been honored in authority outside the home.

---

1. Major British author, essayist, and feminist (1882–1941).

As Margaret Mead[2] has noted, the only women allowed to be dominant and respectable at the same time are widows. You have to do what society wants you to do, have a husband who dies, and then have power thrust upon you through no fault of your own. The whole thing seems very hard on the men.

Before we go on to other reasons why Women's Liberation Is Men's Liberation, too—and why this incarnation of the women's movement is inseparable from the larger revolution—perhaps we should clear the air of a few more myths—the myth that women are biologically inferior, for instance. In fact, an equally good case could be made for the reverse.

Women live longer than men. That's when the groups being studied are always being cited as proof that we work them to death, but the truth is that women live longer than men even when the groups being studied are monks and nuns. We survived Nazi concentration camps better, are protected against heart attacks by our female hormones, are less subject to many diseases, withstand surgery better and are so much more durable at every stage of life that nature conceives 20 to 50 per cent more males just to keep the balance going.

The Auto Safety Committee of the American Medical Association has come to the conclusion that women are better drivers because they're less emotional than men. I never thought I would hear myself quoting the AMA, but that one was too good to resist.

I don't want to prove the superiority of one sex to another: that would only be repeating a male mistake. The truth is that we're just not sure how many of our differences are biological and how many are societal. What we do know is that the differences between the two sexes, like the differences between races, are much less great than the differences to be found within each group.

Chains of Mink

A second myth is that women are already being treated equally in this society. We ourselves have been guilty of perpetuating this myth, especially at upper economic levels where

2. Renowned anthropologist and social activist (1901–1978).

women have grown fond of being lavishly maintained as ornaments and children. The chains may be made of mink and wall-to-wall carpeting, but they are still chains.

The truth is that a woman with a college degree working full time makes less than a black man with a high school degree working full time. And black women make least of all. In many parts of the country—New York City, for instance—a woman has no legally guaranteed right to rent an apartment, buy a house, get accommodations in a hotel or be served in a public restaurant. She can be refused simply because of her sex.

In some states, women get longer jail sentences for the same crime. Women on welfare must routinely answer humiliating personal questions; male welfare recipients do not. A woman is the last to be hired, the first to be fired. Equal pay for equal work is the exception. Equal chance for advancement, especially at upper levels or at any level with authority over men, is rare enough to be displayed in a museum.

As for our much-touted economic power, we make up only 5 per cent of the Americans receiving $10,000 a year or more, and that includes all the famous rich widows. We are 51 per cent of all stockholders, a dubious honor these days, but we hold only 18 per cent of the stock—and that is generally controlled by men.

In fact, the myth of economic matriarchy in this country is less testimony to our power than to resentment of the little power we do have.

You may wonder why we have submitted to such humiliations all these years; why, indeed, women will sometimes deny that they are second-class citizens at all. The answer lies in the psychology of second-classness. Like all such groups, we come to accept what society says about us. We believe that we can make it in the world only by "Uncle Tom-ing," by a real or pretended subservience to white males.

Even when we come to understand that we, as individuals, are not second-class, we still accept society's assessment of our group—a phenomenon psychologists refer to as internalized aggression. From this stems the desire to be the only woman in an office, an academic department or any other part of the man's world. From this also stems women who put down their sisters—and my own profession of journalism has some of them.

Inhumanity to Man

I don't want to give the impression, though, that we want to join society exactly as it is. I don't think most women want to pick up briefcases and march off to meaningless, depersonalized jobs. Nor do we want to be drafted—and women certainly should be drafted; even the readers of *Seventeen* magazine were recently polled as being overwhelmingly in favor of women in national service—to serve in a war like the one in Indochina.

We want to liberate men from those inhuman roles as well. We want to share the work and responsibility, and to have men share equal responsibility for the children. Probably the ultimate myth is that children must have fulltime mothers, and that liberated women make bad ones. The truth is that most American children seem to be suffering from too much mother and too little father.

Women now spend more time with their homes and families than in any other past or present society we know about. To get back to the sanity of the agrarian or joint family system, we need free universal day care. With that aid, as in Scandinavian countries, and with laws that permit women equal work and equal pay, man will be relieved of his role as sole breadwinner and stranger to his own children.

No more alimony. Fewer boring wives. Fewer childlike wives. No more so-called "Jewish mothers," who are simply normally ambitious human beings with all their ambitiousness confined to the house. No more wives who fall apart with the first wrinkle because they've been taught that their total identity depends on their outsides. No more responsibility for another adult human being who has never been told she is responsible for her own life, and who sooner or later says some version of, "If I hadn't married you, I could have been a star." Women's Liberation really Is Men's Liberation, too.

The family system that will emerge is a great subject of anxiety. Probably there will be a variety of choices. Colleague marriages, such as young people have now, with both partners going to law-school or the Peace Corps together, is one alternative. At least they share more than the kitchen and the bedroom. Communes; marriages that are valid for the child-rearing years only—there are many possibilities.

The point is that Women's Liberation is not destroying the American family. It is trying to build a human compassionate alternative out of its ruins.

Simply Incorruptible

One final myth that women are more moral than men. We are not more moral; we are only uncorrupted by power. But until the old generation of male chauvinists is out of office women in positions of power can increase our chances of peace a great deal.

I personally would rather have had Margaret Mead as President during the past six years of Vietnam than either Lyndon Johnson or Richard Nixon. At least she wouldn't have had her masculinity to prove. Much of the trouble this country is in has to do with the masculine mystique: the idea that manhood somehow depends on the subjugation of other people. It's a bipartisan problem.

The challenge to all of us is to live a revolution, not to die for one. There has been too much killing, and the weapons are now far too terrible. This revolution has to change consciousness, to upset the injustice of our current hierarchy by refusing to honor it. And it must be a life that enforces a new social justice.

Because the truth is that none of us can be liberated if other groups are not. Women's Liberation is a bridge between black and white women, but also between the construction workers and the suburbanites, between Mr. Nixon's Silent Majority and the young people it fears. Indeed, there's much more injustice and rage among working-class women than among the much publicized white radicals.

Women are sisters; they have many of the same problems, and they can communicate with each other. "You only get radicalized," as black activists always told us, "on your own thing." Then we make the connection to other injustices in society. The women's movement is an important revolutionary bridge, and we are building it.

The Argument That Won *Roe v. Wade*

Sarah Weddington

On October 11, 1972, twenty-five-year-old attorney
Sarah Weddington appeared before the U.S. Supreme
Court to argue the case of Norma McCorvey—known to
the public as "Jane Roe"—a poor, unmarried young
woman who sought an abortion but was forbidden by
Texas law from having the procedure because her life was
not at risk. Weddington, who volunteered to take Mc-
Corvey's case after a male lawyer turned it down, argued
in her thirty-minute brief to the Supreme Court, excerpted below, that the Fourteenth Amendment's right to
liberty applies to abortion. To deprive women of the right
to make crucial decisions about their futures, she contends, is to deprive them of their right to liberty.

Inciting a storm of controversy that has not died
down to this day, the court ruled on January 22, 1973,
that it was unconstitutional for states to prohibit abortion during the first two trimesters of pregnancy. *Roe v.
Wade* was considered a tremendous victory by most
women's rights activists of the time.

Mr. Chief Justice, and may it please the Court: . . .
In Texas, the woman is the victim. The state
cannot deny the effect that this law has on the
women of Texas. Certainly there are problems regarding even the use of contraception. Abortion now, for a
woman, is safer than childbirth. In the absence of abortions—

From Sarah Weddington, arguments before the U.S. Supreme Court in the case of
Roe v. Wade, December 13, 1971.

or, legal, medically safe abortions—women often resort to the illegal abortions, which certainly carry risks of death, all the side effects such as severe infections, permanent sterility, all the complications that result. And, in fact, if the woman is unable to get either a legal abortion or an illegal abortion in our state, she can do a self-abortion, which is certainly, perhaps, by far the most dangerous. And that is no crime.

Texas, for example, it appears to us, would not allow any relief at all, even in situations where the mother would suffer perhaps serious physical and mental harm. There is certainly a great question about it. If the pregnancy would result in the birth of a deformed or defective child, she has no relief. Regardless of the circumstances of conception, whether it was because of rape, incest, whether she is extremely immature, she has no relief.

I think it's without question that pregnancy to a woman can completely disrupt her life. Whether she's unmarried, whether she's pursuing an education, whether she's pursuing a career, whether she has family problems—all of the problems of personal and family life for a woman are bound up in the problem of abortion.

For example, in our state there are many schools where a woman is forced to quit if she becomes pregnant. In the City of Austin that is true. A woman, if she becomes pregnant, and if in high school, must drop out of the regular education process. And that's true of some colleges in our state. In the matter of employment, she often is forced to quit at an early point in her pregnancy. She has no provision for maternity leave. She has—she cannot get unemployment compensation under our laws, because the laws hold that she is not eligible for employment, being pregnant, and therefore is eligible for no unemployment compensation. At the same time, she can get no welfare to help her at a time when she has no unemployment compensation and she's not eligible for any help in getting a job to provide for herself.

There is no duty for employers to rehire women if they must drop out to carry a pregnancy to term. And, of course, this is especially hard on the many women in Texas who are heads of their own households and must provide for their already existing children. And, obviously, the responsibility of raising a child is a most serious one, and at times an emotional investment that must be made cannot be denied.

Pregnancy Disrupts a Woman's Life

So a pregnancy to a woman is perhaps one of the most determinative aspects of her life. It disrupts her body. It disrupts her education. It disrupts her employment. And it often disrupts her entire family life. And we feel that, because of the impact on the woman, this certainly—in as far as there are any rights which are fundamental—is a matter which is of such fundamental and basic concern to the woman involved that she should be allowed to make the choice as to whether to continue or to terminate her pregnancy.

I think the question is equally serious for the physicians of our state. They are seeking to practice medicine in what they consider the highest methods of practice. We have affidavits in the back of our brief from each of the heads of public—of heads of obstetrics and gynecology departments from each of our public medical schools in Texas. And each of them points out that they were willing and interested to immediately begin to formulate methods of providing care and services for women who are pregnant and do not desire to continue the pregnancy. They were stopped cold in their efforts, even with the declaratory judgment, because of the DA's position that they would continue to prosecute. . . .

[Concerning the constitutionality of the case], in the lower court, as I'm sure you're aware, the court held that the right to determine whether or not to continue a pregnancy rested upon the Ninth Amendment—which, of course, reserves those rights not specifically enumerated to the government to the people. I think it is important to note, in a law review article recently submitted to the Court and distributed among counsel by Professor Cyril Means Jr. entitled "The Phoenix of Abortional Freedom," that at the time the Constitution was adopted there was no common-law prohibition against abortions, that they were available to the women of this country. . .

[And] insomuch as members of the Court have said that the Ninth Amendment applies to rights reserved to the people, and those which were most important—and certainly this is—that the Ninth Amendment is the appropriate place insofar as the Court has said that life, liberty, and the pursuit of happiness involve the most fundamental things of people; that this matter is one of those most fundamental matters. I think, in as far as the Court has said there is a penumbra that exists to encompass the entire purpose of the Constitution, I think one of the purposes of the Constitution was to guarantee to individuals the right to determine the course of their own lives.

The Women's Movement Is Incompatible with Family Life

Phyllis Schlafly

Although the women's liberation movement was lauded for its progress in expanding women's career and educational opportunities, not all women believed that the movement was an overall positive force. One of the most fervent opponents of the women's liberation movement was conservative activist Phyllis Schlafly. A lawyer and mother of six children, Schlafly became the leader of the pro-family movement, which championed the traditional family model.

Speaking to an audience of Southern Baptists in Orlando, Florida, in 1979, Schlafly denounces the women's liberation movement as a major cause of divorce and other societal problems. She claims that the movement, by promoting the belief that women are victims of male oppression, creates hostility between the sexes. Furthermore, she asserts, the feminist tenet that women should seek self-fulfillment is completely incompatible with the demands of marriage and motherhood. Schlafly proposes the Positive Women's Movement, which affirms the value of women's role as a homemaker, as an alternative to the women's liberation movement.

From Phyllis Schlafly, speech delivered at a convention of Southern Baptists in Orlando, Florida, in 1979. Reprinted with permission from the author.

Good morning friends. The subject assigned today is, indeed, an important one: the women's movement and family life. It is important that we first of all define the term. I would not agree that there is just *the* women's movement. In order to make sure we know what we are talking about, I will first of all describe what I think could be more appropriately called the women's liberation movement. It could be defined as the movement of women who have, in a general way, been working for the Equal Rights Amendment.

This movement was born in the mid-1960s with the publication of Betty Friedan's book *The Feminine Mystique*. This movement accomplished the task of getting the Equal Rights Amendment through Congress in 1972. It reached its peak in November 1977 in Houston at the National Conference of the Commission on International Women's Year. Since that date, it's no longer a nebulous thing. It is a very precise movement that can be definitely defined with particular people and particular goals.

Participating in that Houston Conference were all the leaders of the women's liberation movement. These included the head of the National Organization for Women (NOW), the head of the Women's Political Caucus, the head of ER-America (the lobbying group for the ERA), the head of the Gay Task Force, the person who put the ERA through the Senate, the person who put ERA though the House, Gloria Steinem, and Bella Abzug was the chairman. These were all presidential appointees, and they gathered in Houston. They had $5 million of federal funds and they passed twenty-five resolutions, which represent the goals of the women's liberation movement.

The four "hot button" issues, the term used by *Newsweek* magazine—their most important goals—were ratification of the Equal Rights Amendment, government-funded abortion, lesbian privileges to be recognized with the same dignity as husbands and wives and with the right to teach in schools, and massive, universal, federal child care, which *Time* magazine estimated would cost us an additional $25 billion a year. There were other resolutions, too, but the four "hot button" issues were admitted by everybody—the media plus both sides—as being the main ones.

An Adverse Effect on Family Life

These are the goals and those are the personalities of the women's liberation movement in our country today. It is my belief, based on working with this movement for quite a number of years, that the movement is having an adverse effect on family life, that it is a major cause of divorce today, and that it is highly detrimental to our country and to our families. . . .

For a woman to function effectively in the family, it is necessary for her to believe in the worth of her position, to have a certain amount of self-esteem, to believe that her task as wife and mother is worthy, is honorable, is useful, and is fulfilling. The fundamental attitude by the women's liberation movement takes all that away from women. I have listened to thousands of their speeches, and basically those speeches inculcate in woman a negative attitude toward life, toward the family, toward their country, and most of all toward themselves. It was best summed up in an advertisement developed by the principal women's liberation organization, the National Organization for Women. It was run as a spot announcement on many television stations and as ads in many magazines and newspapers. This advertisement shows a darling, curly-headed child. The caption under the picture is: "This normal, healthy child was born with a handicap. It was born female."

Think about that. That is the startling assumption of the woman's liberation movement: That somebody—it isn't clear who, God or the establishment or a conspiracy of male chauvinist pigs—has dealt women a foul blow by making them female; that it is up to society to remedy these centuries of oppression, of bondage, even of slavery. Women are told that they are not even persons in our society. They are told that they are second-class citizens. I have given speeches where women have been picketing up and down outside, wearing placards saying, "I am a second-class citizen." I feel so sorry for women who are deliberately inculcating this inferiority complex. Women are not second-class citizens in our society. Whatever women may have been hundreds of years ago, in other lands, or in other countries, that is not the condition of women in our country today.

The thesis of the speeches that women's liberation movement speakers are giving runs basically like this: "Sister, when you wake up in the morning, the cards are stacked against you. You won't get a job, and if you get one, it won't be a good one. You'll never be paid what you're really worth. You won't be promoted as you deserve to be. You simply will never get a fair break in our society. And if you get married, your husband will treat you like a servant, like a chattel"—that's one of their favorite words—"and life is nothing but a bunch of dirty diapers and dirty dishes."

It's no wonder that women have problems when they listen to that line. The women's liberation movement literature is the greatest put-down of women that anything could possibly be. It's difficult to pick yourself up off the floor after you have listened to those tirades about how women are kept in bondage and enslaved, and how the home is a cage or a prison from which women must be liberated. This line creates a natural hostility between men and women. No longer are men people with whom we work in harmony. Men are the enemy who must make it up to us for these centuries of injustice.

Whatever lowly status women may endure in other lands, that is not the situation of American women. It is also true that nobody in this world who wakes up in the morning with a chip on your shoulder, whether it is man or woman, is going to have a happy or fulfilling life, or get ahead in this world.

This is not to say that there aren't any problems. The world is full of problems. I don't know anybody who doesn't have problems. Women face all kinds of problems: husbands out of a job, handicapped children, senile parents, or not enough money. The world is full of problems. But you don't solve your problems by waking up in the morning with a chip on your shoulder, believing and telling yourself hour after hour that you've been oppressed, and that it is up to somebody to remedy years of injustice.

The "New Narcissism"

After having flattened women by spreading this negative attitude, the women's liberation movement then comes along and offers its solution. The solution can be best described as the "new narcissism." You remember the story of Narcissus: the Greek youth who fell in love with his own image in the reflecting pool and finally died of unrequited desire.

The women's liberation movement teaches women this fundamental approach to life: "Seek your own self-fulfillment over every other value." It's a free country for those who choose to establish their scale of values that way. Some women make that choice, and they are free to do so if that is what they want. But I simply have to tell women that *that* attitude, that choice of goals, is not compatible with a happy marriage. It is *not* compatible with a successful family life and it is *not* compatible with motherhood.

In order to live in harmony in family life, with a man who's been brought up in another environment, you have to make social compromises, and most of us think that marriage is worth the price.

Motherhood must be a self-sacrificing role, a role of dedication and service. The mother must be able to subordinate her self-fulfillment and her desire for a career to the well-being of her children so that she can answer her child's call any hour of the day or night. This is what marriage and motherhood are all about, and it is not compatible with the dogmas of the women's liberation movement.

The women's liberation movement preaches that the greatest oppression of women is that women get pregnant and men don't get pregnant, and so women must be relieved of this oppression! The second greatest oppression of women, according to the liberation movement, is that society expects mothers to look after their babies, that society reduces women to this menial, tedious, tiresome, confining, repetitive chore of looking after babies.

Well, I suppose it's all in your point of view. Many of us believe that the ability to participate in the creation of human life is the great gift that God gave to women. The task of taking care of babies, despite its tedious drudgery, is better than most of the jobs of the world. Women should find out how exhausting most of the rest of the jobs of the world are. Besides, a mother has something to show for her efforts after twenty years: You've got a living, breathing human being, a good citizen, a wonderful human being you've given to this world.

But the women's movement is causing wives with relatively good families to walk out. Women's lib is a dogma that is especially contagious among women in their forties and fifties after their children are in school. Wives who "catch" the disease of women's liberation are walking out on marriage—not because of the traditional problems in marriage such as alcohol, or money, or adultery, but just to seek their own self-fulfillment.

I speak almost every week on college campuses and I see these abandoned teenagers. Young women come up to me and say, "My mother has left. What can you say to my mother, who has brought up four children and now thinks her whole life is wasted?" The women who "catch" women's liberation are walking out. It makes no difference whether they're northern and eastern liberal homes or southern and western conservative homes. Once they get this message, they go out into emptiness, abandoning their families.

This women's liberation dogma is also very contagious among young college women. They have bought a large part of it. The biggest thing that hits you on the college campuses today is that the educated young women of our nation are rejecting marriage and motherhood. Most important, they're rejecting motherhood. They're saying that if they have a baby, they don't want it to interfere with their careers. I have young men coming to me now saying that they want to marry a young woman, but she tells them very frankly, "If we have a baby, I'm not going to let that baby interfere with my career. I see nothing the matter with putting the baby in some child-care facility at the age of three or four weeks." Remember, this is not a matter of need. These are not hungry people. These are a class of women who expect to have degrees but they don't want that baby to interfere with their careers. Of course, my answer to those young men is, "Forget her." A woman who is unwilling to take care of her own baby is a pathetic sight, and there's nothing in marriage for a man to have a relationship like that. This is what the women's liberation movement is doing to the young women of our nation. . . .

There *is* another women's movement. You don't hear much about it, but I believe it is more powerful. It is the Positive Woman's Movement: the woman who knows who she is. The Positive Woman is not searching for her identity. She knows God made her, she knows why she's here, and she has her scale of values in order. This movement was born in 1972 when some of us realized we had to protect ourselves against the takeaway of the legal rights of the homemaker that was embodied in the Equal Rights Amendment. This movement showed itself at the marvelous Pro-Family Rally in Houston in 1977 where 15,000 people came at their own expense—not like the other one where people came at the taxpayers' expense. Our movement of Positive Women came of age on March 22, 1979 in Washington, D.C., when we celebrated, at a marvelous dinner in Washington, the expiration of the seven years that was set as the time period for ratification of the Equal Rights Amendment. . . .

Our Positive Women are not seeking their own self-fulfillment as the highest value, as the women's liberation movement tries to teach women. Our Positive Women are dedicated to service, to faith and trust in God, to the family, and to this great country that we have been fortunate enough to live in. We are not seeking to get our bit at the price of taking benefits away from others, as the woman's liberation movement is doing. We have taken on these great odds, believing, as we are told in II Chronicles, "Be not afraid, nor dismayed by reason of the great multitude, for the battle is not yours but God's."

We have fought the greatest political forces that anybody has ever fought in our country in this century. We have won, with God's help, because we are Positive Women. We don't wake up in the morning mad at anybody. We have women who are talented, articulate, capable. We have lady legislators and successful career women. We have some who are solely successful career women, others who are wives and mothers but who are also successful in an auxiliary career. The great thing about woman's role is that she can have different careers at different times in her life. But our Positive Women have their scale of values in order: no matter what they may seek for their own self-fulfillment, they know that the family is more important.

Our women are, I believe, the greatest positive force in our country today. We believe that we can do great things.

Now that we move into the more positive phase of our activity, we will work for the restoration of the family unit, which is coming apart at the seams in many areas. We want to show women how, in this great country, women can do whatever they want and have all kinds of exciting lives. But for a woman to be a successful wife and mother, during that period of her life, marriage and motherhood must come first over selfish values.

In conclusion, I share with you the comment attributed to a French writer who traveled our country in another century and wrote many commentaries which are still studied in our schools. When he came to the conclusion of his travels, Alexis de Tocqueville wrote, "I sought for the greatness and genius of America in her commodious harbors and ample rivers, but it was not there. I sought for the greatness of America in her fertile lands and boundless prairies, but it was not there. It was not until I went into the churches of America and found her pulpits aflame with righteousness that I understood the secret of her genius and her power. America is great because America is good, and if America ever ceases to be good, she will cease to be great." The Positive Women of America are pledging themselves to do our part to make sure that America continues to be good.

CHAPTER
FOUR

GREAT
SPEECHES
IN
HISTORY

Contemporary Speeches on Women's Rights

Promoting the Human Rights of Women

Charlotte Bunch

Although American and European women have achieved
equality in most aspects of life, women in many other
parts of the world are still second-class citizens who suffer discrimination and sometimes even persecution. In
Afghanistan, for example, women are required by Tal-
iban law to wear a shroud that covers their entire body
and face; in parts of Africa, girls must undergo the horri-
fying ritual of genital mutilation. In some Muslim societies, women cannot work, own property, or even drive a
car without their husbands' permission.

The women's rights movement has been active in criticizing these egregious injustices. During the last two
decades, women's rights leaders have united with human
rights organizations to establish international conferences
on women, designed to raise awareness of the oppression
faced by women all over the world. At one of these conferences, held in 1995 in Beijing, China, Charlotte Bunch
outlined the global problems facing women in the twenty-
first century, arguing that fundamentalist religions pose
the most serious threat to women's autonomy. In her
speech, excerpted here, she maintains that women's rights
should be regarded as an issue of human rights; as human
beings, she contends, women deserve the right to freedom
of religion and speech, as well as freedom from violence.

Charlotte Bunch, an activist in the women's and civil
rights movements since the 1960s, was inducted into the

From Charlotte Bunch, "Through Women's Eyes: Global Forces Facing Women in
the Twenty-first Century," speech delivered at the Center for Women's Global Leadership NGO Forum '95, August 31, 1995. Reprinted by permission of the author.

Women's Hall of Fame in 1996. She has edited seven an-
thologies and co-authored the book *Demanding Accountability: The Global Campaign and Vienna Tribunal for
Women's Human Rights.* In 1989, Bunch founded the
Center for Women's Global Leadership at Douglass College, Rutgers University, where she currently serves as director and professor of urban studies.

T his conference is occurring at a critical juncture in
time throughout the world because it is a time of transition—a time when the ways of governing, the ways
of living and of doing business, the ways of interacting
amongst people and nations are in flux. In my region, Europe
and North America, which has a long history of war and
domination that has affected the entire globe, we see this
transition in what is called the end of the Cold War. We have
now what I call the hot peace. Rather than a truly peaceful
era, we are seeing a shift in power blocs in which the antici-
pated peace dividend has turned instead into increased racial,
ethnic, religious and gender-based conflicts and violence. In
this escalation, the role of women—questions of women's
human rights and the violation of women as a symbol of
their cultures and peoples—has become central.

These global changes are offering both opportunity and
danger for women, as in any time of crisis. The opportunity is
there for women to offer new solutions, to enter the public
policy debate in a way that we have never been able to do before. And the danger is that even those advances we have made
in this century will be reversed if we are not able to take this
opportunity to move forward. When I talk about women entering the global policy debates and influencing those discussions, I don't see this as totally separate from, but rather building on, the work that women are already doing. Women are
usually the leaders at the local community level. Women are
the leaders who have held families and communities together
in times of crisis. Women have managed budgets that were inadequate to raise children and have managed to keep people
together in times of war and other conflicts. And yet, as power

moves up the ladder from that local community to national and international policy making, women's voices and women themselves disappear. It is precisely a movement to change this that women have begun in the last two decades—we have begun to demand a place at the table of global policy making as well as at the table in the kitchen. The incredible failures of international policy in this century make it clear that women's expertise and experience must be brought to the global agenda if we are to see change in the 21st century. Let me give one poignant example—Somalia. For many years during the various conflicts there, women preserved the communities and sustained daily life as they have in many other conflict situations. Yet when efforts were made to seek peace, these women were not given any role. They were not recognized as important to the future. The international community did not bring them into the peace-making negotiations, did not ask them to participate in the peace-keeping process. I believe that if these women had been legitimized by the United Nations, by my own government and by other governments in the world, then we would have seen a different resolution to that country's problems. And so too in many other parts of the world.

While there is much talk these days around the United Nations about global governance, there is not yet talk about global governance that includes our half of the population. But in reality we already have a form of global governance in the world. We have an undeclared, unaccountable governance by the global economy with the IMF [International Monetary Fund] and the World Bank and various military alliances making the basic decisions that govern our lives. The other speakers have described the impact this has in the third world in terms of structural adjustment policies. I would like to add that in the North we see the dismantling of social welfare in both formerly socialist countries and in the West, which is structural adjustment in our part of the world. This dismantling of social welfare has the same impact as structural adjustment in that it sacrifices human needs and human rights for economic expediency. And it is women who suffer the most in all of our countries from these policies because it is women who must make up for the services lost to family and community.

Both economic and cultural life are becoming more global as they are more dominated by global market values. Even in my own lifetime in the United States, which probably seems very homogenous to most of you, I have seen the erasure of distinct geographical diversity and cultural variations in the process of the creation of a common MacWorld of consumerist culture that sacrifices difference. And now I see that process being transported throughout the world. Women have to find a better way for the world to have development and find common ground while still retaining cultural and other forms of diversity.

While we have a global economy and a growing global culture, we have no effective global political structures for overseeing these processes. On the contrary, in the world today, we are facing two polar opposites; we are told we either have to accept the global economy with its homogenized consumerist culture or we have to return to "traditional" cultural patterns and life. I believe that women must devise a third way, a third option.

Reactionary Forces

On the traditional side, we see groups that are reacting against the global economy and their lack of control over their economic life by clinging to local identities which involve more and more narrow definitions of who they are and what they are about. We see the growth of a narrow nationalistic ethnic fragmentation into separatist enclaves where all "others" are demonized and seen as less than human. This is obviously expressed in ethnic cleansing in the former Yugoslavia or in the ethnic battles in Rwanda. But it is also present in the neo-fascist, white supremacist forces that are rising in the United States, France, Germany and many other countries in my region.

Another form of such reaction is the rise of religious fundamentalist movements that take a narrow patriarchal view of religion, whether Muslim, Christian, Hindu, Jewish or others. These movements often cross national lines and sometimes become global forces, but they too are based on a narrow call for identity that dehumanizes "the other" as those who are not members of their religious group. And therefore, the identity, the commonality that is developed is in opposition to and seeks domination over others, rather than building a spirit of solidarity, of humanity and tolerance for those not like oneself.

These conservative reactionary forces, whether nationalistic or religious or both, all seek to control women. This control is absolutely central to religious or ethnic or cultural purity and identity. If they cannot control the women, they cannot ensure purity of race and identity, and in that very key point lies the vulnerability and potential strength of women. Women must refuse these narrow definitions and say that there can be diverse cultures and ethnic identities living together, that there can be tolerant religions that don't have to be in opposition to the other, that we can live in solidarity and respect with those who are different. If women do this, we can be the key to denying narrow fundamentalist movements their source of power and source of regeneration. In this area, women must speak more forcefully about how we are being manipulated, and we must redefine this debate and create the third force that I mentioned earlier.

Another reason women are key is that many of the fundamentalist forces see the family, women, and culture as areas that they can control even when they can't control global economic forces. This has fueled the conservative backlash against women's autonomy and against all minority "others" who might live differently, such as immigrants, gypsies, lesbian and gay people, etc. This brings us to the question of the very definition of the family. Feminists have been accused of being anti-family, but the conservative forces have continually narrowed the understanding of what the family really is. Women must point out that we are pro-family, but we are pro-democratic, pluralistic, non-violent, tolerant families that are based on respect for the human rights of all. Such families do not form the basis for narrow ethnic enclaves which will fight other families and other ethnic groups but instead create the basis for family members who respect minorities and other groups.

The same forces that seek to return women to narrow definitions of our role in the family solely as reproducers and caretakers of the race are agitating against the rights of minorities, whether racial, ethnic or religious groups, gay and lesbian minorities, gypsies and immigrants. Whoever gets defined as "the other" in your culture, that is part of the way in which all of our humanity is destroyed. If we accept that any group is less than fully human and therefore deserves to have fewer human rights, we have started down the slope of losing human rights for all. And women especially should understand this. After all, as women, we live in a male-defined world where we are still the original "other," and most of the definitions of issues and approaches in this world do not fit our experience.

For example, many of us have worked for the last few years to transform the definitions and interpretations of human rights so that they will recognize the reality of the violations that women experience every day. The original terminology of human rights as we know it today came initially from the experience of the white propertied European/American male who did not need to worry about violence in the family or poverty because those were not his problems. His human rights needs, where he felt his humanity was most violated was in relation to the state, in terms of matters such as his right to freedom of religion and speech. While these issues are also important to women and other groups around the world, we have had to seek a redefinition of human rights that acknowledges that the first fundamental of all human rights is the right to exist, the right to life itself. This requires looking at the right to food and the right to freedom from violence both in the home and in the streets. Of course women also need the right to freedom from violence from the state. But many women do not even get to the point where the state is the problem because they are still so oppressed in their homes and by the economy that they are often unable to take political actions which might put them into human rights conflict in the political sphere.

This work on human rights is part of the process of redefining what women are doing in relation to all the fundamental questions of our global order—of democracy, development, environment, peace, etc. We must look at these questions from the point of view of women's lives and from the point of view of all of those who have been marginalized by the dominant paradigm and definitions of these concepts. In this way we begin to pose alternatives, to move toward a model of society that is not based on domination and alienation and the divisiveness that we see in the world today.

The challenge in terms of human rights is to find a model that shows one can have respect for the common humanity and universality of the human rights of every person regardless of gender, race, ethnicity, religion, sexual orientation, age, disability, etc., while also respecting and creating space for the incredible multicultural diversity that exists among us so that everyone doesn't have to become like the dominant group in order to have rights. Human rights is not static but is an evolving concept that responds to how people see their human needs and dignity over time. Thus as people exercise their human right to self-determination there will always be a dynamic process of both expanding the concept and ensuring that the exercise of rights does not allow for domination over others.

Involving Women in the Human Rights Dialogue

Women's involvement in this human rights dialogue is part of the process of breaking away from the polarization that the global economy has brought on between moving back to the past to preserve identity or moving to the future simply by accepting the values and domination of the global economy. Women must become more involved in seeking to develop global democratic structures for global governance and in demanding accountability and respect for human rights from those bodies like the United Nations that are engaged in these conversations. Because the United Nations itself is the ultimate expression of male domination, it can hardly become the body that will create global governance that respects women's human rights. That is, not unless it too changes. So as we enter into this NGO [non-governmental organizations] Forum and send our messages back to Beijing to the government conference, one of those messages has to be that women in the world are watching the United Nations. We are watching, and the UN itself is on trial here. We are watching to see whether the UN can become the governing body from which we develop global democratic structures of governance that fully include women or whether indeed, we will have to go elsewhere.

Seeing the importance of the recognition of women's human rights and the need of all these nationalistic and fundamentalist movements to control women's sexuality, reproduction, and labor helps us understand why this conference and the Cairo conference are under so much attack. These events represent women's efforts to move into the global arena, to have a voice, to become a global force that must be reckoned with. When I look at the list of the global forces that we are to speak about today, I realize the one most important to me is the global force of women in movement around the world today. This global force of women around the world has many different names, call it feminist, call it womanist, call it women in development, call it women's rights or women's human rights. Call it many different things because each of us has found different terms that describe best for us that reality of domination and change. Women are the most important new global force on the horizon in the world today with the potential to create a more humane future and a humane global governance.

For women to be such a force, however, carries great responsibility. We can not be a movement that thinks and speaks only from our own experiences. We began our movement in this past few decades with the concept that the personal is political and with the need to put women's experiences on the agenda because these were missing. Women's issues, women's perspectives, women's experiences were and still often are left out of policy deliberations. But if we don't want to be simply an added-on dimension, we must also bring in all those whose voices are not heard—all the diverse women and men whose voices have been muted—so that we show it is possible for this world to hear from all its peoples. There will be conflicts, but we must seek non-violent ways to resolve them that move toward the future and away from the militaristic models of domination that the world operates from today. . . .

In this process of empowering women to become greater actors in shaping our societies, women's human rights are key in many ways. Perhaps the simplest way to put this is, how can leaders talk about creating a democratic, sustainable development or a culture of peace and respect for human rights in public life if there is still pervasive denial of development and violation of the human rights of half of humanity in private life? The violence and domination of women that prevails at the core of society in the family undermines any talk of such goals. I believe that it is this connection that women have understood. The public and the private are not separate spheres. As long as we teach violence and domination at the core in our homes and allow them to permeate children's lives from the beginning, we are never going to be able to end the militarism and violence that dominates other relations around differences of race or religion or nationality. Children are taught very early to accept domination based on differences and to see violence as an acceptable solution to conflict and to believe that they have to be either victims or the conquerors. To alter such a dynamic and this violence in public life requires eliminating it in private life as well.

I want to add that I think the United States has a severe problem in its cultural tradition of violence. We often refer to cultural traditions as if they only existed in the third world. One of the traditions of the United States is a tradition of violence. This violence extends from the family to the media to our sport stars to our militarization around the world. And it is this cultural tradition that we must counter in our region just as women from other regions challenge the domination of women in their cultural traditions. So I ask that we never again make the mistake of talking about culture and tradition as if they did not apply to every country and every region of the world when we speak of the changes necessary for the achievement of women's human rights.

Finally, at this conference, we must take one step further into the global arenas of this decade. I think of these UN world conferences as global town meetings. They are opportunities where we meet and talk to each other across the lines of nationality, across lines that we don't often have other opportunities to cross. But as global town meetings, they are also occasions for us to show the world our visions. Looking at the world through women's eyes is an excellent slogan for this forum because this is the place where we can demonstrate the visions of possibility that come from women. . . . We believe the world can be transformed by looking at it through women's eyes. In so doing, we are opening ever wider the horizon so that what gets onto the global stage, into the Internet, and onto that CNN television screen reflects more of reality and more of what women believe can be done for change. So we put the UN and the governments on trial not only this week, but this year and this decade. We are participating now, we are watching, we are demanding, and we are here to see if this can become the arena of real participation where global governance and policies can be created with a human face that is both male and female and where all the diversity of both male and female can emerge. And if this does not prove possible, women must say to the United Nations and to all of our governments, that we have a vision for the future and that is where we are going. We hope that they will allow us to participate and to lead. If they don't, we will take leadership anyway and show that the world can be better for all in the twenty-first century.

The Status of Women in Islamic Nations

Benazir Bhutto

In December 1988, Benazir Bhutto became the first female leader of an Islamic nation when she was sworn in
as the prime minister of Pakistan. She is the daughter of
former Pakistani leader Zulfikar Ali Bhutto, who in 1977
was ousted from power by the military regime and
hanged. This same regime also arrested Benazir Bhutto
on several occasions during the 1980s for taking part in
anti-government activities. In 1986, bolstered by public
support, Bhutto demanded that General Zia Ul-Haq step
down as the leader of Pakistan. The following month she
and her mother were elected co-chairwomen of the Pakistan People's Party; not long afterwards, Bhutto was
elected prime minister.

During her reign as prime minister, from 1988–1990
and again from 1993–1997, Bhutto worked to provide
food for the hungry, health care, jobs, and a monthly
minimum wage. In a speech delivered at the 1995 world
conference on women held in Beijing, excerpted below,
Bhutto addresses the oppression of women in Muslim societies. Bhutto, herself a Muslim, argues that such societies must return to the original tenets of Islam, which
support democracy, tolerance, and women's equality.
Commentator William Safire describes Bhutto's speaking
style as "well-modulated but forthright, well-mannered
with a touch of defiance."

From Benazir Bhutto, speech delivered to the U.N. Fourth World Conference on
Women, Beijing, China, September 1995.

As the first woman ever elected to head an Islamic nation, I feel a special responsibility about issues that relate to women.

In addressing the new exigencies of the new century, we must translate dynamic religion into a living reality. We must live by the true spirit of Islam, not only by its rituals. And for those of you who may be ignorant of Islam, cast aside your preconceptions about the role of women in our religion.

Contrary to what many of you may have come to believe, Islam embraces a rich variety of political, social, and cultural traditions. The fundamental ethos of Islam is tolerance, dialogue, and democracy.

Just as in Christianity and Judaism, we must always be on guard for those who will exploit and manipulate the Holy Book for their own narrow political ends, who will distort the essence of pluralism and tolerance for their own extremist agendas.

The Ethos of Islam

To those who claim to speak for Islam but who would deny to women our place in society, I say:

The ethos of Islam is equality, equality between the sexes. There is no religion on earth that, in its writing and teachings, is more respectful of the role of women in society than Islam.

My presence here, as the elected woman prime minister of a great Muslim country, is testament to the commitment of Islam to the role of women in society.

It is this tradition of Islam that has empowered me, has strengthened me, has emboldened me.

It was this heritage that sustained me during the most difficult points in my life, for Islam forbids injustice; injustice against people, against nations, against women.

It denounces inequality as the gravest form of injustice.

It enjoins its followers to combat oppression and tyranny.

It enshrines piety as the sole criteria for judging humankind.

It shuns race, color, and gender as a basis of distinction amongst fellowmen.

When the human spirit was immersed in the darkness of the Middle Ages, Islam proclaimed equality between men and women. When women were viewed as inferior members of the human family, Islam gave them respect and dignity.

When women were treated as chattels, the Prophet of Islam (*Peace Be Upon Him*) accepted them as equal partners.

Islam codified the rights of women. The *Koran* elevated their status to that of men. It guaranteed their civic, economic, and political rights. It recognized their participative role in nation building.

Sadly, the Islamic tenets regarding women were soon discarded. In Islamic society, as in other parts of the world, their rights were denied. Women were maltreated, discriminated against, and subjected to violence and oppression, their dignity injured and their role denied.

Women became the victims of a culture of exclusion and male dominance. Today more women than men suffer from poverty, deprivation, and discrimination. Half a billion women are illiterate. Seventy percent of the children who are denied elementary education are girls.

Women in Developing Countries

The plight of women in the developing countries is unspeakable. Hunger, disease, and unremitting toil is their fate. Weak economic growth and inadequate social support systems affect them most seriously and directly.

They are the primary victims of structural adjustment processes which necessitate reduced state funding for health, education, medical care, and nutrition. Curtailed resource flows to these vital areas impact most severely on the vulnerable groups, particularly women and children.

This, Madam Chairperson, is not acceptable. It offends my religion. It offends my sense of justice and equity. Above all, it offends common sense.

That is why Pakistan, the women of Pakistan, and I personally have been fully engaged in recent international efforts to uphold women's rights. The Universal Declaration of Human Rights enjoins the elimination of discrimination against women.

The Nairobi Forward Looking Strategies provide a solid framework for advancing women's rights around the world. But the goal of equality, development, and peace still eludes us.

Sporadic efforts in this direction have failed. We are satisfied that the Beijing Platform of Action encompasses a comprehensive approach toward the empowerment of women. This is the right approach and should be fully supported.

Women cannot be expected to struggle alone against the forces of discrimination and exploitation. I recall the words of Dante, who reminded us that "The hottest place in Hell is reserved for those who remain neutral in times of moral crisis."

Today in this world, in the fight for the liberation of women, there can be no neutrality.

My spirit carries many a scar of a long and lonely battle against dictatorship and tyranny. I witnessed, at a young age, the overthrow of democracy, the assassination of an elected prime minister, and a systematic assault against the very foundations of a free society.

But our faith in democracy was not broken. The great Pakistani poet and philosopher Dr. Allama Iqbal says, "Tyranny cannot endure forever." It did not. The will of our people prevailed against the forces of dictatorship.

Democracy Is Not Enough

But, my dear sisters, we have learned that democracy alone is not enough.

Freedom of choice alone does not guarantee justice.

Equal rights are not defined only by political values.

Social justice is a triad of freedom, an equation of liberty:

Justice is political liberty.
Justice is economic independence.
Justice is social equality.

Delegates, sisters, the child who is starving has no human rights.

The girl who is illiterate has no future.

The woman who cannot plan her life, plan her family, plan a career, is fundamentally not free. . . .

I am determined to change the plight of women in my

country. More than sixty million of our women are largely sidelined.

It is a personal tragedy for them. It is a national catastrophe for my nation. I am determined to harness their potential to the gigantic task of nation building. . . .

I dream of a Pakistan in which women contribute to their full potential. I am conscious of the struggle that lies ahead. But, with your help, we shall persevere. Allah willing, we shall succeed.

Let Women All Rise Together

Angela Y. Davis

As a doctoral candidate in philosophy at the University of
California at San Diego in the late 1960s, Angela Y.
Davis became a member of the Communist Party and the
Black Panthers. Due to her associations with these radical
groups, Davis was under surveillance by the U.S. government; furthermore, in 1970 the University of California
Board of Regents refused to renew her appointment as a
lecturer in philosophy, despite her excellent teaching
record at UCLA. That same year, Davis was charged with
conspiring to free revolutionary George Jackson in a
shootout in Marin County, California, and became the
third woman to appear on the FBI's most wanted list. After evading the police for two weeks, Davis was discovered in New York City and arrested. She spent sixteen
months in prison before she was acquitted of all charges.

After her release from prison, Davis published several
books: a collection of her essays, entitled *If They Come
in the Morning: Voices of Resistance*; *Angela Davis: An
Autobiography*; and *Women, Race, and Class*. Upon its
publication in 1981, the latter book was considered an
exemplar of feminist scholarship. Today, Davis is a
tenured professor at the University of California at Santa
Cruz and a frequent lecturer on politics, race, and
women's rights. In a speech given to the National
Women's Studies Association annual conference in 1987,
excerpted here, Davis criticizes the early women's movement for failing to address the needs of poor and minority women. If contemporary feminists want to help all

From Angela Y. Davis, "Radical Perspectives on Empowerment for Afro-American
Women: Lessons for the 1980s," *Harvard Educational Review*, vol. 58, no. 3
(August 1988), pp. 348–53. Copyright © 1988 by the President and Fellows of
Harvard College. Reprinted with permission. All rights reserved.

women, Davis contends, they must "lift as they climb"—
that is, they must work to guarantee that all women, regardless of class or race, have equal rights and adequate
protection of those rights under the law.

The concept of empowerment is hardly new to Afro-
American women. For almost a century, we have been
organized in bodies that have sought collectively to
develop strategies illuminating the way to economic and political power for ourselves and our communities. During the
last decade of the nineteenth century, after having been repeatedly shunned by the racially homogeneous women's
rights movement, Black women organized their own Club
Movement. In 1895—five years after the founding of the
General Federation of Women's Clubs, which consolidated a
club movement reflecting concerns of middle-class White
women—one hundred Black women from ten states met in
the city of Boston, under the leadership of Josephine St.
Pierre Ruffin, to discuss the creation of a national organization of Black women's clubs. As compared to their White
counterparts, the Afro-American women issuing the call for
this national club movement articulated principles that were
more openly political in nature. They defined the primary
function of their clubs as an ideological as well as an activist
defense of Black women—and men—from the ravages of
racism. When the meeting was convened, its participants em-
phatically declared that, unlike their White sisters, whose or-
ganizational policies were seriously tainted by racism, they
envisioned their movement as one open to all women:

> Our woman's movement is woman's movement in that it is
> led and directed by women for the good of women and
> men, for the benefit of *all* humanity, which is more than
> any one branch or section of it. We want, we ask the ac-
> tive interest of our men, and, too, we are not drawing the
> color line; we are women, American women, as intensely
> interested in all that pertains to us as such as all other
> American women; we are not alienating or withdrawing,
> we are only coming to the front, willing to join any others

in the same work and cordially inviting and welcoming any others to join us.[1]

The following year, the formation of the National Association of Colored Women's Clubs was announced. The motto chosen by the Association was "Lifting as We Climb."[2]

The nineteenth-century women's movement was also plagued by classism. Susan B. Anthony wondered why her outreach to working-class women on the issue of the ballot was so frequently met with indifference. She wondered why these women seemed to be much more concerned with improving their economic situation than with achieving the right to vote.[3] As essential as political equality may have been to the larger campaign for women's rights, in the eyes of Afro-American and White working-class women it was not synonymous with emancipation. That the conceptualization of strategies for struggle was based on the peculiar condition of White women of the privileged classes rendered those strategies discordant with working-class women's perceptions of empowerment. It is not surprising that many of them told Ms. Anthony, "Women want bread, not the ballot."[4] Eventually, of course, working-class White women, and Afro-American women as well, reconceptualized this struggle, defining the vote not as an end in itself—not as the panacea that would cure all the ills related to gender-based discrimination—but rather as an important weapon in the continuing fight for higher wages, better working conditions, and an end to the omnipresent menace of the lynch mob.

"Lifting as We Climb"

Today, as we reflect on the process of empowering Afro-American women, our most efficacious strategies remain those that are guided by the principle used by Black women in the club movement. We must strive to "lift as we climb." In other words, we must climb in such a way as to guarantee that all of our sisters, regardless of social class, and indeed all of our brothers, climb with us. This must be the essential dynamic of our quest for power—a principle that must not only determine our struggles as Afro-American women, but also govern all authentic struggles of dispossessed people. Indeed, the overall battle for equality can be profoundly enhanced by embracing this principle.

Afro-American women bring to the women's movement a strong tradition of struggle around issues that politically link women to the most crucial progressive causes. This is the meaning of the motto, "Lifting as We Climb." This approach reflects the often unarticulated interests and aspirations of masses of women of all racial backgrounds. Millions of women today are concerned about jobs, working conditions, higher wages, and racist violence. They are concerned about plant closures, homelessness, and repressive immigration legislation. Women are concerned about homophobia, ageism, and discrimination against the physically challenged. We are concerned about Nicaragua and South Africa. And we share our children's dream that tomorrow's world will be delivered from the threat of nuclear omnicide. These are some of the issues that should be integrated into the overall struggle for women's rights if there is to be a serious commitment to the empowerment of women who have been rendered historically invisible. These are some of the issues we should consider if we wish to lift as we climb.

During this decade we have witnessed an exciting resurgence of the women's movement. If the first wave of the women's movement began in the 1840's, and the second wave in the 1960's, then we are approaching the crest of a third wave in the final days of the 1980's. When the feminist historians of the twenty-first century attempt to recapitulate the third wave, will they ignore the momentous contributions of Afro-American women, who have been leaders and activists in movements often confined to women of color, but whose accomplishments have invariably advanced the cause of White women as well? Will the exclusionary policies of the mainstream women's movement—from its inception to the present—which have often compelled Afro-American women to conduct their struggle for equality outside the ranks of that movement, continue to result in the systematic omission of our names from the roster of prominent leaders and activists of the women's movement? Will there continue to be two distinct continuums of the women's movement, one visible and another invisible, one publicly acknowledged and

another ignored except by the conscious progeny of the
working-class women—Black, Latina, Native American,
Asian, and White—who forged that hidden continuum? If
this question is answered in the affirmative, it will mean that
women's quest for equality will continue to be gravely defi-
cient. The revolutionary potential of the women's movement
still will not have been realized. The racist-inspired flaws of
the first and second waves of the women's movement will
have become the inherited flaws of the third wave.

Creating a Revolutionary, Multiracial Women's Movement

How can we guarantee that this historical pattern is broken?
As advocates and activists of women's rights in our time, we
must begin to merge that double legacy in order to create a
single continuum, one that solidly represents the aspirations
of all women in our society. We must begin to create a revolutionary, multiracial women's movement that seriously addresses the main issues affecting poor and working-class
women. In order to tap the potential for such a movement, we
must further develop those sectors of the movement that are
addressing seriously issues affecting poor and working-class
women, such as jobs, pay equity, paid maternity leave, feder-
ally subsidized child care, protection from sterilization abuse,
and subsidized abortions. Women of all racial and class backgrounds will greatly benefit from such an approach.

For decades, White women activists have repeated the
complaint that women of color frequently fail to respond to
their appeals. "We invited them to our meetings, but they
didn't come." "We asked them to participate in our demonstration, but they didn't show." "They just don't seem to be
interested in women's studies."

This process cannot be initiated merely by intensified efforts to attract Latina women or Afro-American women or
Asian or Native American women into the existing organiza-
tional forms dominated by White women of the more privileged economic strata. The particular concerns of women of
color must be included in the agenda.

An issue of special concern to Afro-American women is

unemployment. Indeed, the most fundamental prerequisite for empowerment is the ability to earn an adequate living. At the height of its audacity, the Reagan government boasted that unemployment had leveled off, leaving only (!) 7.5 million people unemployed. These claims came during a period in which Black people in general were twice as likely to be unemployed as White people, and Black teenagers almost three times as likely to be unemployed as White teenagers.[5] We must remember that these figures do not include the millions who hold part-time jobs, although they want and need full-time employment. A disproportionate number of these underemployed individuals are women. Neither do the figures reflect those who, out of utter frustration, have ceased to search for employment, nor those whose unemployment insurance has run out, nor those who have never had a job. Women on welfare are also among those who are not counted as unemployed.

At the same time that the Reagan administration attempted to convey the impression that it had successfully slowed the rise of unemployment, the AFL-CIO [The American Federation of Labor and Congress of Industrial Organizations] estimated that 18 million people of working age were without jobs. These still-critical levels of unemployment, distorted and misrepresented by the Reagan administration, are fundamentally responsible for the impoverished status of Afro-American women, the most glaring evidence of which resides in the fact that women, together with their dependent children, constitute the fastest-growing sector of the 4 million homeless people in the United States. There can be no serious discussion of empowerment today if we do not embrace the plight of the homeless with an enthusiasm as passionate as that with which we embrace issues more immediately related to our own lives.

The United Nations declared 1987 to be the Year of Shelter for the Homeless. Although only the developing countries were the initial focus of this resolution, eventually it became clear that the United States is an "undeveloping country." Two-thirds of the 4 million homeless in this country are families, and 40 percent of them are Afro-American.[6] In some urban areas, as many as 70 percent of the homeless are Black.

In New York City, for example, 60 percent of the homeless population are Black, 20 percent Latino, and 20 percent White.[7] Presently, under New York's Work Incentive Program, homeless women and men are employed to clean toilets, wash graffiti from subway trains, and clean parks at wages of sixty-two cents an hour, a mere fraction of the minimum wage.[8] In other words, the homeless are being compelled to provide slave labor for the government if they wish to receive assistance.

Black women scholars and professionals cannot afford to ignore the straits of our sisters who are acquainted with the immediacy of oppression in a way many of us are not. The process of empowerment cannot be simplistically defined in accordance with our own particular class interests. We must learn to lift as we climb.

Organized Resistance to Racist Violence

If we are to elevate the status of our entire community as we scale the heights of empowerment, we must be willing to offer organized resistance to the proliferating manifestations of racist violence across the country. A virtual "race riot" took place on the campus of one of the most liberal educational institutions in this country not long ago. In the aftermath of the World Series, White students at the University of Massachusetts, Amherst, who were purportedly fans of the Boston Red Sox, vented their wrath on Black students, whom they perceived as a surrogate for the winning team, the New York Mets, because of the predominance of Black players on the Mets. When individuals in the crowd yelled "Black bitch" at a Black woman student, a Black man who hastened to defend her was seriously wounded and rushed unconscious to the hospital. Another one of the many dramatic instances of racist harassment to occur on college campuses during this period was the burning of a cross in front of the Black Students' Cultural Center at Purdue University.[9] In December 1986, Michael Griffith, a young Black man, lost his life in what amounted to a virtual lynching by a mob of White youths in the New York suburb of Howard Beach. Not far from Atlanta, civil rights marchers were attacked on Dr.

Martin Luther King's birthday by a mob led by the Ku Klux Klan. An especially outrageous instance in which racist violence was officially condoned was the acquittal of Bernhard Goetz, who, on his own admission, attempted to kill four Black youths because he *felt* threatened by them on a New York subway.

Black women have organized before to oppose racist violence. In the nineteenth century the Black Women's Club Movement was born largely in response to the epidemic of lynching during that era. Leaders like Ida B. Wells and Mary Church Terrell recognized that Black women could not move toward empowerment if they did not radically challenge the reign of lynch law in the land. Today, Afro-American women must actively take the lead in the movement against racist violence, as did our sister-ancestors almost a century ago. We must lift as we climb. As our ancestors organized for the passage of a federal antilynch law—and indeed involved themselves in the woman suffrage movement for the purpose of securing that legislation—we must today become activists in the effort to secure legislation declaring racism and anti-Semitism as crimes. Extensively as some instances of racist violence may be publicized at this time, many more racist-inspired crimes go unnoticed as a consequence of the failure of law enforcement to specifically classify them as such. A person scrawling swastikas or "KKK" on an apartment building may simply be charged—if criminal charges are brought at all—with defacing property or malicious mischief. Recently, a Ku Klux Klanner who burned a cross in front of a Black family's home was charged with "burning without a permit." We need federal and local laws against acts of racist and anti-Semitic violence. We must organize, lobby, march, and demonstrate in order to guarantee their passage.

As we organize, lobby, march, and demonstrate against racist violence, we who are women of color must be willing to appeal for multiracial unity in the spirit of our sister-ancestors. Like them, we must proclaim: We do not draw the color line. The only line we draw is one based on our political principles. We know that empowerment for the masses of women in our country will never be achieved as long as we do not succeed in pushing back the tide of racism. It is not a coincidence that sexist-inspired violence—in particular, terrorist attacks on abortion clinics—has reached a peak during the same period in which racist violence has proliferated dramatically. Violent attacks on women's reproductive rights are nourished by these explosions of racism. The vicious antilesbian and antigay attacks are a part of the same menacing process. The roots of sexism and homophobia are found in the same economic and political institutions that serve as the foundation of racism in this country and, more often than not, the same extremist circles that inflict violence on people of color are responsible for the eruptions of violence inspired by sexist and homophobic biases. Our political activism must clearly manifest our understanding of these connections. . . .

When we as Afro-American women, when we as women of color, proceed to ascend toward empowerment, we lift up with us our brothers of color, our White sisters and brothers in the working class, and, indeed, all women who experience the effects of sexist oppression. Our activist agenda must encompass a wide range of demands. We must call for jobs and for the unionization of unorganized women workers, and, indeed, unions must be compelled to take on such issues as affirmative action, pay equity, sexual harassment on the job, and paid maternity leave for women. Because Black and Latina women are AIDS victims in disproportionately large numbers, we have a special interest in demanding emergency funding for AIDS research. We must oppose all instances of repressive mandatory AIDS testing and quarantining, as well as homophobic manipulations of the AIDS crisis. Effective strategies for the reduction of teenage pregnancy are needed, but we must beware of succumbing to propagandistic attempts to relegate to young single mothers the responsibility for our community's impoverishment.

In the aftermath of the Reagan era, it should be clear that there are forces in our society that reap enormous benefits from the persistent, deepening oppression of women. Members of the Reagan administration include advocates for the most racist, antiworking class, and sexist circles of contemporary monopoly capitalism. These corporations continue to prop up apartheid in South Africa and to profit from the spiraling arms race while they propose the most vulgar and irrational forms of anti-Sovietism—invoking, for example, the "evil empire" image popularized by Ronald Reagan—as justifications for their omnicidal ventures. If we are not afraid to adopt a revolutionary stance—if, indeed, we wish to be radical in our quest for change—then we must get to the root of our oppression. After all, *radical* simply means "grasping things at the root." Our agenda for women's empowerment must thus be unequivocal in our challenge to monopoly capitalism as a major obstacle to the achievement of equality.

I want to suggest, as I conclude, that we link our grassroots organizing, our essential involvement in electoral politics, and our involvement as activists in mass struggles to the long-range goal of fundamentally transforming the socioeconomic conditions that generate and persistently nourish the various forms of oppression we suffer. Let us learn from the strategies of our sisters in South Africa and Nicaragua. As Afro-American women, as women of color in general, as progressive women of all racial backgrounds, let us join our sisters—and brothers—across the globe who are attempting to forge a new socialist order—an order which will reestablish socioeconomic priorities so that the quest for monetary profit will never be permitted to take precedence over the real interests of human beings. This is not to say that our problems will magically dissipate with the advent of socialism. Rather, such a social order should provide us with the real opportunity to further extend our struggles, with the assurance that one day we will be able to redefine the basic elements of our oppression as useless refuse of the past.

Speaker's Footnotes

1. Gerda Lerner, *Black Women in White America* (New York: Pantheon Books, 1972), p. 443.

2. These clubs proliferated the progressive political scene during this era. By 1916—twenty years later—50,000 women in 28 federations and over 1,000 clubs were members of the National Association of Colored Women's Clubs. See Paula Giddings's discussion of the origins and evolution of the Black Women's Club Movement in *When and Where I Enter* (New York: William Morrow, 1984), Chapters IV–VI.

3. Miriam Schneier, ed., *Feminism: The Essential Historical Writings* (New York: Vintage, 1972), pp. 138–42.

4. Ibid.

In Support of *Roe v. Wade*

Kate Michelman

Although the right to a legal abortion was affirmed by
the 1973 Supreme Court decision in *Roe v. Wade*, abortion continues to be a focal issue for contemporary feminists. As retiring Supreme Court justices are replaced
with new appointees, many women fear that the *Roe v.
Wade* decision will be overturned. Others argue that it
should be: A recent wave of vociferous female activists,
who are sometimes collectively referred to as "postfeminists," strongly oppose abortion.

Kate Michelman, pro-choice leader for more than two
decades, has been the president of the National Abortion
and Reproductive Rights Action League since 1985 and
previously served as Executive Director of Planned Parenthood in Harrisburg, Pennsylvania. In the following
speech, delivered to the Commonwealth Club of California in 1998, Michelman explains why abortion rights are
still at risk. She asserts that a woman's right to a legal
abortion is a fundamental freedom that must be defended.

L yndon Johnson died in Texas on January 22, 1973—
the same day *Roe v. Wade* was handed down in Washington. I was in Pennsylvania—mothering three young
daughters. I remember the next day's front pages giving ex-
pansive coverage to the dead president—sadly overshadow-
ing this most historic victory for women.

I remember reading of the promise—and the trajectory—

From Kate Michelman, speech delivered to the Commonwealth Club of California,
San Francisco, January 15, 1998. Reprinted with permission.

of the Johnson presidency. Begun in the chaos of assassination—then reaching great heights with passage of civil rights and the advent of the Great Society—and finally falling back into the darkness of Vietnam.

And I remember the sense of triumph reading about *Roe*. The promise that emerged from darkness into the light. From despair to hope.

Back then, I understood better than most what *Roe* really meant for women. Because it came too late for me. Too late for my abortion. And too late for so many women—and so many tragedies—that came before me.

It was 1970—the year *Roe* came to court. I was a young mother with three daughters under the ages of five. My life was my family. Then one day my husband left. I was terrified. Suddenly I was alone in my responsibility to my children. I was a homemaker with no money, no job, no car. I was quickly forced onto welfare.

Then—almost immediately after my husband left—I found I was pregnant. I was devastated. Physically, financially, emotionally—I couldn't care for another child.

Like most women, I never expected to even consider an abortion. I was a Catholic woman. Abortion was illegal. It was shrouded in shame and wrapped in danger. I couldn't discuss abortion with my mother, my sister or my friends—let alone my priest. I had to struggle with the moral and ethical questions alone—to debate my obligations to my children against my responsibility to the developing life inside me. In the end, I chose my children. I chose abortion.

But in those days, that was not a choice I could make by myself. I had to appear before an all-male hospital board. They asked all the awful questions. They probed into the most intimate details of my life. I felt completely worthless, violated. The only way I could get a safe, legal abortion—the only way I could avoid putting myself at risk—was to convince them that I was unstable—that I was incapable of raising another child—that I was unfit to be a mother.

But the inquisition had a final—and most demeaning—twist. The board finally agreed to grant me an abortion—but, first, I had to get written permission from the man who abandoned me and our daughters.

I found him. He gave me permission. And I had the abortion.

So, when *Roe* was handed down, I was quite overcome. It felt somehow like a benediction—a retroactive reprieve that helped restore my sense of worth, my integrity. Finally, so many thousands of ordinary women—women in crisis, women in despair—had been pardoned for our "crimes"— we had finally been elevated to true citizenship.

Elevated by one of the most fundamental precepts ever written into law. Right alongside the freedom to worship. Right alongside the freedom to vote. The freedom to choose.

The Magnitude of *Roe v. Wade*

Twenty-five years ago. *Roe v. Wade.* Like all judgements of that magnitude—at first, an abstraction. A principle. Wrapped in great American values. Liberty. Equality. Trust. So large, and so filled with potential, that most women—especially those who were to benefit the most—could not grasp it at once.

That each woman had the legal right to end a pregnancy. That no woman would ever again be forced to risk her life or her fertility with a back alley abortion. That every woman could openly talk to her doctor about abortion—and have one. A legal one. A safe one. That government would remain neutral—remain remote—in our decision whether or not to end a pregnancy. No one had the power to interfere with this most intimate and personal of choices. Not the president. Not the Congress. Not the courts. Not the bureaucrats.

Roe v. Wade. Suddenly, an entire legal history of prejudice had been turned on its head. Suddenly, women in crisis—and the doctors who helped them—were no longer criminals. A new civil right had been granted. A new tolerance had been demanded. And a new moral debate had begun.

In the end, *Roe v. Wade* was as much about the past as about the future. It was as much an indictment—as much an apology—as it was a promise. It was an indictment of our blindness not to see into the heart and mind of every woman. An indictment of a people who doubted a woman's personal sense of responsibility. It was an apology to the millions of women who were bound to live in despair for lack of any legal, safe means to prevent unwanted children—an apology to those who died breaking the law. In a larger sense, it was an apology—come very late—that women were never acknowledged in our original Constitution.

For all of us—for all women—*Roe* was the last legal stop—the final judgement that reproductive choice is critical to women's full continued progress toward full and equal participation in American life. It was a national promise—a federal guarantee—that was ours forever and ever. Forever and ever, we could count on the right to choose—with privacy, with dignity. Forever and ever, we had control of our reproductive decisions. Forever and ever, we would live without fear—without violation—without humiliation.

From the darkness of back alley abortions to the brilliance of Constitutional freedom, every woman's status as a citizen was guaranteed. Finally, a woman's right to choice was acknowledged as a fundamental American right. Finally, conscience was assigned to women.

How wrong we were.

Still Fighting Battles

Twenty-five years later, we're still fighting battles we thought were won that day. Defending ground that had long been ours. Twenty-five years later, we're still up against intolerance and intimidation.

Women suffer harassment outside clinics. Doctors are killed and their families threatened—doctors performing the most common surgery in America—doctors doing fetal tissue research at universities like Yale—trying to find cures for Hodgkin's, Alzheimer's, Parkinson's. Some are denied malpractice insurance—and research grants—as punishment. Shareholders turn on corporations that give to organizations involved with reproductive rights.

Twenty-five years later we're still up against the same zealous forces that denied us liberty for so long. Up against the same intolerance and arrogance that drive forward their cause to take back a woman's freedom to choose.

They are the radical right—the Christian Coalition—Pat

Robertson—they are the Catholic bishops. They are members of the United States Congress. They govern statehouses. They write state laws. They preach from the pulpit. They sit in county courthouses. They are elected to boards of education and hospital boards.

Roe's promise to women of the right to choose an abortion free of state interference before fetal viability remains under constant siege.

Of 435 representatives in the House, only 131 are pro-choice. In the Senate, they number 33. Our opponents chair most of the committees that have jurisdiction over reproductive rights and women's health. They control much of the machinery that determines what bills get an open vote—and what bills never make it to the floor. Since 1995, we've faced 81 votes to limit reproductive choice. We lost all but 10.

Abortion has become a lever to control legislation that has nothing to do with reproductive choice. Witness Congressman Chris Smith from New Jersey who recently held hostage a bill to fund the United Nations—demanding that the United States pull back funds from all international family planning programs. Foreign policy played against the right to choose.

Whether it's the high profile debate on late term abortion—or the ban on fetal tissue research—this Congress continues to reopen the most fundamental questions answered in *Roe*. Who should decide whether or not to have a child? Who should be the final arbiter in her choice? Pat Robertson? Newt Gingrich? Jesse Helms? A federal bureaucrat? A county judge?

Or a woman? A woman and her doctor.

Our opponents are as sophisticated as they are willful. They've learned not to attack *Roe* directly. They don't have the White House. They don't yet have the votes on the Supreme Court. They don't have a majority of voters.

So they come at *Roe* from the flanks. They come to cripple *Roe*. They know the impact of sensationalism. They battle against the right to choose with insidious efforts to shock and alarm the public. They calculated the impact of graphic and exaggerated description of third trimester abortions. They counted on shocking mainstream Americans into ambivalence over abortion.

It is that ambivalence that has given the radical right such recent success at the polls. Their target is moderate voters in both parties—those who support *Roe*'s core protection—but who are seduced into accepting restrictions at the margins of *Roe*. It is that uncertainty—that ambivalence—that has given rise to an election strategy that was born in Oregon, and successfully used in Virginia's recent gubernatorial race. The message is pure deception: First, concede that *Roe* is the law of the land—and isn't going to be overturned. Then ask for a few "safeguards," as they call them, like bans on third-trimester abortion.

So voters who are pro-choice have a candidate's guarantee that *Roe* will remain the law of the land. And, after all the sensationalism and horror stories paraded out by the right wing, moderate voters too often accept a few so-called "safeguards" around the edges.

Well, these "safeguards" have gone a long way to cripple *Roe*—to make abortion more complicated and less accessible for women at risk.

Four years ago, Chief Justice Rehnquist put it bluntly: "*Roe* continues to exist, but only in the way a storefront on a western movie set exists: a mere facade to give the illusion of reality."

In state houses from Maine to Arizona we're forced to fight a steady assault of anti-choice legislation—405 bills introduced last year—all raising a cruel barrier between women in crisis—and the guarantee of *Roe*. Through waiting periods. Parental consent. State-mandated lectures. Simple harassment—simple intimidation—simple obstruction. All aimed at taking back *Roe*—except by name. All aimed at taking America back to a time when women were just expected to bear and raise children—a time when sexuality was hidden and unspoken—a time of intolerance. A time before *Roe*.

The real victims of this strategy? The silent women—remote from government. Silent women who don't expect help—silent women who don't march. Too often they're women with little income—and even less education. Women who live in the remotest corners of America—and in our inner cities. African American, Native American, Latina, White.

They're teenagers. New to sexuality. Driven by peer pressure and fantasy. Looking for recognition. Completely un-ready to raise a child—unprepared for the cost—unable to give it a secure home.

How we respond to these silent women—how we re-spond to the millions of women of child-bearing age—rests on who we really are—what we really believe is the Ameri-can way. Abortion is not the question. The question is values. The value we put on a woman. The value we put on her choice to bear a child. The value we put on rearing that child.

A Fundamental Right at Stake

Our struggle today is about much more than keeping abor-tion legal. It's about protecting a right that is so fundamental to us as a people. A woman's complete freedom to measure and decide when the circumstances are right to bring a child into the world—and when they are not. A right that is cen-tral to all rights that express the integrity of person and indi-vidual conscience.

I am reminded that Eleanor Roosevelt was once asked, "Where do rights begin?" She replied: "in small places, close to home—so close and so small they cannot be seen on any map of the world. Yet they are in the world of the individual person—where every man, woman and child seeks equal jus-tice, equal opportunity, equal dignity, without discrimina-tion. Unless rights have meaning there, they have little mean-ing everywhere."

It's that fundamental right—that profound freedom— that's at stake today. Whether or not a woman—alone—has complete freedom to make these most intimate decisions. The very essence of womanhood—who we are—is our free-dom to choose what we believe is right. How can we women ever hope to take an equal place in America if we aren't given that respect—if we aren't trusted? Without interrogations. Without indignities. Without violence.

Tell me.

As long as the radical right succeeds in fixating America with the act of abortion—they succeed in diverting us—in preventing us all from moving beyond the fundamental guar-antees of *Roe*—to the critical fight for a country committed to bringing up healthy, secure children. As long as they keep NARAL [National Abortion and Reproductive Rights Action League] and others like us defending the right to an abortion, they obscure and delay national focus on the larger pro-choice mission.

They prevent us from giving women the support to make the best choice—to do everything we can to ensure women's decisions are informed decisions—to reduce crisis pregnancies—to spare unwanted children. To make abortion less necessary.

Our job is to give men and women the means to manage their reproductive lives. To teach our children how to avoid unintended pregnancy, to make available contraception, to provide the health care that help women carry wanted, healthy pregnancies to term.

That we, as a nation, have failed to respond to this dramatic need is starkly evident.

Today most agree that 60 percent of all pregnancies are unintended. That's three million unintended pregnancies a year, including one million teenage pregnancies—half of which end in abortion. This is not just a problem facing teenagers or unmarried women. An estimated 40 percent of all pregnancies to married women are unintended.

Compound these dramatic statistics by inevitable poverty, crime, illiteracy and the cost goes far higher.

We must move beyond abortion. We must focus on the lack of a coherent national policy on sexual and reproductive health—and begin the massive task of rebuilding America's human infrastructure.

Our leaders talk about investing in the future. If the most critical investment we can make isn't to bring into this world healthy, wanted, secure children—then what is it? We can talk about education. We can talk about putting people to work. About safe streets. The goals of a society. But society begins in a single moment—the moment that a woman becomes pregnant. Who we are—what we become as a nation—hangs on our concern for that decision—on our preparation for that moment.

A healthy society comes down to whether we have educated our young to make responsible choices. Whether we have prepared them to understand their own sexuality. Whether we have taught them the consequences of having sex. Whether we have adequately explained the connection between having a family—and supporting a family. Whether we can guarantee sound health care for those women who choose to have a child—before and after birth. That's the measure of an intelligent and caring people.

Clearly, the nation needs to do more to reduce the need for abortion. We must refocus national policy to guarantee access—to tear down the barriers—to contraception and family planning. It means making new demands on our research scientists. It means educating women on the use of emergency contraceptive pills. They're legal—they're safe—they're effective—and they're virtually unknown.

According to one survey, only one percent of women at risk for unplanned pregnancies have used ECPs. Sixty-eight percent of these women are unaware that anything can be done to prevent pregnancy after intercourse. Just think of that—in 1998.

Yet, I'm still optimistic about what the turn of the century will bring to America. A higher trajectory. We look forward to more effective prevention and remedies for cancer and AIDS. We look forward to a broader peace around the world. To stronger economies. To greater democracy.

Yet, sadly, American women will probably leave this century still fighting for a freedom that we thought we had won 25 years ago. We are frustrated to be still fighting the same indignities, the same intolerance, the same rigidity that gave birth to *Roe*. We wonder at having to defend this most basic of human freedoms.

"Life, liberty and the pursuit of happiness" ring hollow without a deeper national commitment to choice.

In the 1973 *Roe v. Wade* opinion, Justice Harry Blackmun foresaw that many public and political leaders would not universally embrace *Roe*. He wrote that "abortion raises moral and ethical questions over which honorable persons can disagree sincerely and profoundly. But their disagreements did not then and do not now relieve us of our duty to apply the Constitution faithfully."

Justice Blackmun understood where rights begin. He foresaw that 25 years later we would still be fighting battles we thought were won in 1973, defending ground that long had been ours. Perhaps we were naive. Today, however, we are seasoned advocates for choice.

We understand where rights begin. We understand that they are fragile and must be constantly protected, defended, and promoted. We recognize that the political will to protect choice seems to slip and slide as the years go by. Opponents of choice are determined, well-organized and well-financed. They fight hard and are willing to go beyond disagreement and rational debate. They have undermined the fact that choice is inextricably linked to all rights guaranteed by our Constitution.

But we know where rights begin. NARAL pledges to all pro-choice people and to our opposition that we will continue. Our cause is just and right and will prevail in the 21st century.

We will prevail by doubling our efforts to protect choice.

Today we celebrate *Roe*—we pay our respects to the court—we applaud our early pro-choice pioneers—we acknowledge the politicians and political leaders who against great odds have voted their conscience, and we mourn the wasted lives of women who suffered and died before *Roe*.

I appeal to all pro-choice people to renew your commitment to *Roe*.

We have barriers to cross and battles ahead. We stand firm and ready to fight and prevail. *Roe v. Wade* is our legacy: our daughters, granddaughters and their daughters must enjoy the right to choice.

Only if we act together—promise to stay in the fray so that choice remains a fundamental American value and right—can we cross safely into the next century.

The Feminist Case Against Abortion

Serrin M. Foster

Early feminists such as Susan B. Anthony and Elizabeth Cady Stanton condemned abortion as a type of infanticide. Feminists of the 1960s, on the other hand, adopted abortion rights as one of their main causes, arguing that women's equality depended on women's ability to control their own reproduction.

Contemporary women's rights activists fall into two categories: those who believe that abortion rights are essential to women's independence, and those who feel that abortion harms women. Feminists for Life (FFL), an organization whose mission is to eliminate the causes that drive women to seek abortions, represents the latter group. Serrin M. Foster, president of FFL, explains in the following speech why the pro-life position is a feminist one. She argues that women have abortions because they lack financial resources and emotional support; abortion, she maintains, is a symptom of—but not a solution to—women's unequal status in society. Foster encourages people to put aside their ideological differences on abortion and work to help pregnant women in need. Foster delivered "The Feminist Case Against Abortion" on various occasions in 1999 and 2000 to enthusiastic audiences comprised of both pro-life and pro-choice supporters.

T he feminist movement was born more than two hundred years ago when Mary Wollstonecraft wrote *A Vindication of the Rights of Woman*. After decrying

From Serrin M. Foster, "The Feminist Case Against Abortion," *The Commonwealth*, September 13, 1999. Reprinted with permission.

the sexual exploitation of women, she condemned those who would "either destroy the embryo in the womb, or cast it off when born." Shortly thereafter, abortion became illegal in Great Britain.

The now revered feminists of the 19th century were also strongly opposed to abortion because of their belief in the worth of all humans. Like many women in developing countries today, they opposed abortion even though they were acutely aware of the damage done to women through constant child-bearing. They opposed abortion despite knowing that half of all children born died before the age of five. They knew that women had virtually no rights within the family or the political sphere. *But they did not believe abortion was the answer.*

Without known exception, the early American feminists condemned abortion in the strongest possible terms. In Susan B. Anthony's newsletter, *The Revolution*, abortion was described as "child murder," "infanticide," and "foeticide." Elizabeth Cady Stanton, who in 1848 organized the first women's rights convention in Seneca Falls, New York, classified abortion as a form of infanticide and said, "When you consider that women have been treated as property, it is degrading to women that we should treat our children as property to be disposed of as we see fit."

Anti-abortion laws enacted in the latter half of the 19th century were a result of advocacy efforts by feminists who worked in an uneasy alliance with the male-dominated medical profession and the mainstream media. The early feminists understood that, much like today, women resorted to abortion because they were abandoned or pressured by boyfriends, husbands and parents and lacked financial resources to have a baby on their own.

Ironically, the anti-abortion laws that early feminists worked so hard to enact to protect women and children were the very ones destroyed by the *Roe v. Wade* decision 100 years later—a decision hailed by the National Organization for Women (NOW) as the "emancipation of women."

The goals of the more recent NOW-led women's movement with respect to abortion would have outraged the early feminists. What Elizabeth Cady Stanton called a "disgusting and degrading crime" has been heralded by Eleanor Smeal, former president of NOW and current president of the Fund for a Feminist Majority, as a "most fundamental right."

Betty Friedan, credited with reawakening feminism in the 1960's with her landmark book, *The Feminine Mystique,* did not even mention abortion in the early edition. It was not until 1966 that NOW included abortion in its list of goals. Even then abortion was a low priority.

How Abortion Became a Feminist Issue

It was a man—abortion rights activist Larry Lader, who remains active today—who credits himself with guiding a reluctant Friedan to make abortion an issue for NOW. Lader had been working to repeal the abortion laws based on population growth concerns, but state legislators were horrified by his ideas. (Immigration and improved longevity were fueling America's population growth—not reproduction, which in fact had declined dramatically.)

Lader teamed up with a gynecologist, Bernard Nathanson, to co-found the National Alliance to Repeal Abortion Laws, the forerunner of today's National Abortion and Reproductive Rights Action League (NARAL).

Lader suggested to the NOW leadership that all feminist demands (equal education, jobs, pay, etc.) hinged on a woman's ability to control her own body and procreation. After all, employers did not want to pay for maternity benefits or lose productivity when a mother took time off to care for a newborn or sick child. Lader convinced the NOW leadership that legalized abortion was the key to the workplace.

Dr. Nathanson, who later became a pro-life activist, states in his book, *Aborting America,* that the two were able to convince Friedan that abortion was a civil rights issue. Later he admitted that they simply made up the numbers of women dying from illegal abortions, which had been a major point in their argument.

Lader's and Nathanson's strategy was highly effective. NOW has made the preservation of legal abortion its number one priority. Its literature repeatedly states that access to abortion is "the most fundamental right of women, without which all other rights are meaningless."

With this drastic change, a highly visible faction of the women's movement abandoned the vision of the early feminists: a world where women would be accepted and respected as women. There are now 1.3 million surgical abortions per year in the United States. The Alan Guttmacher Institute (the research arm of Planned Parenthood) reports that women have abortions for two primary reasons: lack of financial resources and lack of emotional support.

A Symptom of, Not a Solution to, Women's Struggles

Feminists for Life of America recognizes that abortion is a symptom of, not a solution to, the continuing struggles women face in the workplace, at home and in society. Our emphasis is on addressing root causes and promoting solutions—from prevention to practical resources.

The first step is to empower young women and men to make life-affirming choices. No compassionate person, pro-choice or pro-life, wants to see a teenage girl drop out of school and face a lifetime of poverty because she became pregnant. Nor do we want her to suffer the pain and anguish of abortion. Public and private funding for comprehensive programs that emphasize teen pregnancy prevention must be increased dramatically. We need honest and unbiased evaluation and replication of effective programs that include proven strategies such as life-planning skills training and mentoring. Boys, as well as girls, should be included in the remedy.

Groups like Feminists for Life and pregnancy resource centers regularly get calls from women who are pressured by partners who say they will pay $300 for an abortion but won't pay a dime in child support. Men and boys need to know that, thanks to legislation supported by Feminists for Life and other women's organizations that strengthens child support enforcement and paternity establishment, they can no longer coerce women into having an abortion by threatening to abandon their children if they are born. But fathers need to do more than make payments. Their presence is needed in their child's life. For women whose partners are absent and who are unable to provide for their children, assistance must come from both private and public sources to protect children by providing the basis, including affordable, quality child care, and education and employment opportunities for the mother.

If we are serious as a nation about significantly reducing the number of abortions, then established, credible pregnancy resource centers should be eligible for federal funding. Nearly 4,000 pregnancy care centers and maternity homes guide women in crisis through the maze of available support services—food, clothing, housing, furniture, medical care including high risk pregnancies, legal assistance, help with employment and education, drug abuse and domestic violence counseling, childbirth, breast-feeding and parenting classes— all at no charge. Some specialize in bilingual/bicultural services, adoption and/or post-abortion counseling. These centers are where many pro-lifers "walk their talk" to help women in need. They leverage financial and in-kind resources from individuals, businesses, churches and communities across the country, yet they cannot consistently meet the demand for services.

Although these centers are clearly listed in the yellow pages as "abortion alternatives," some abortion advocates have resorted to calling them "fake clinics" to discredit their efforts to give women choices other than abortion. Coercive techniques, lies, and other unethical practices should not be tolerated in abortion clinics or in pregnancy resource centers. While the vast majority of pregnancy resource centers such as those affiliated with Catholic Charities and Birthright, and the vast majority of not-for-profit abortion providers do not engage in these unethical practices—some for-profit abortion clinics and unaffiliated pregnancy care centers may stray from the ethical path. NARAL is currently working to expose those anti-abortion centers that resort to lies and lurid pictures; NARAL should also expose those abortion clinics that try to convince women they have no choices other than abortion.

One model program is First Resort of California. Founder Shari Plunkett approached HMO Kaiser Permanente with a plan to reduce the number of abortions in the Bay area. After thoroughly reviewing the program—even editing brochures—Kaiser agreed to refer clients who were unsure about having an abortion to First Resort. Kaiser's client satisfaction rate was 99.3%. When NARAL's California affiliate (CARAL) succeeded in pressuring Kaiser to terminate the program, women lost the ability to make an informed choice. CARAL ignored an invitation to meet with staff and tour First Resort.

The Right to Know

Across the country, Americans on both sides of the abortion debate agree that women have a right to make informed decisions about their pregnancy. We can empower women to exercise this right by passing "Right to Know" legislation. As with any other medical procedure, women have a right to full disclosure of the nature of the abortion procedure, risks and potential complications and alternative support services, as well as the father's responsibility. A woman has the right to know her doctor's name, whether he/she will be available if a medical emergency emerges, any history of malpractice in any state or revocation of a medical license; she has the right to a fully equipped clinic and/or ambulance nearby in case of complications, and the right to redress if she is hurt by the abortion. Even veterinary clinics are better regulated than abortion clinics, for which there are no uniform inspections or reporting requirements. Doctors who have botched abortions, caused infertility or death and lost their medical licenses have been known to jump state lines to continue providing abortions and even open new clinics. There are no regulations to stop them.

Employers and educational institutions can also implement policies that ensure meaningful options for pregnant and parenting women (as well as parenting men). Women in the workplace should not have to choose between their child and their job. That is no choice at all. Employers who have not already done so should consider flex time, job sharing, on-site child care and telecommuting. Women need maternity coverage in health care; men and women need parental leave. Living wages would enable parents to support their children.

Similarly, women should not be forced to choose between their education and life plans and their child. As Feminists for Life has expanded its College Outreach Program in recent years, a number of college counselors have told us the only choice they are aware of is between various abortion clinics—as if women are not capable of reading or thinking while they are pregnant or parenting. Feminists for Life is leading forums on college campuses that challenge university officials to provide housing, on-site child care and maternity coverage within student health care plans, and inform women about their hard-won right to child support. We have developed comprehensive Pregnancy Resources Kits with the input of those on both sides of the debate—including abortion doctors, pro-choice clinic staff, attorneys and students— to give women the "rest of the choices."

Even though Feminists for Life has reached out to pro-choice activists to help provide more choices for women, ironically, Planned Parenthood, the nation's largest abortion provider, has called Feminists for Life's solution-oriented program "anti-choice."

If providing practical resources that help women can be called "anti-choice," something has gone terribly wrong. It is time to set aside the rhetoric and horror stories and fund-raising tactics and think again about how we can help women in need.

On the 150th Anniversary of the First Women's Rights Convention

Hillary Rodham Clinton

Former First Lady and current U.S. senator from New York, Hillary Rodham Clinton has inspired great admiration, as well as scathing criticism, since her emergence on the national scene. A graduate of Yale Law School, where she met Bill Clinton, Hillary worked as a high-powered attorney in Little Rock, Arkansas, while her husband served for twelve years as governor of the state. In 1991, the *National Law Journal* named her as one of the 100 most influential lawyers in America.

Upon her husband's election to the presidency in 1992, Clinton did not assume the traditional role of the First Lady. Instead, she became extremely active in government affairs—so much so that some referred to her as the "First Partner." In 1993, Clinton led the National Task Force on Health Care, a failed attempt to reform the health care industry to provide coverage for all Americans. She was also a vocal advocate for human rights, the economic empowerment of women across the globe, affordable child care, and an improved foster care system. In the year 2000 Clinton became the first First Lady to be elected senator, winning New York's Democratic seat in one of the most highly publicized Senate battles in U.S. history.

Clinton has spoken frequently on the subject of women's rights, emphasizing the need for a global femi-

From Hillary Rodham Clinton, speech delivered at the 150th anniversary of the first women's rights convention, Seneca Falls, New York, July 16, 1998.

nist agenda aimed at helping women in undeveloped nations. Here, in a speech delivered in Seneca Falls, New York, Clinton commemorates the 150th anniversary of the first women's rights convention, held in that same city in 1848. In this speech, Clinton reflects on the successes of the women's rights movement. However, she argues, if the movement is to complete its work, it must strive to eliminate wage discrimination, provide affordable child care and health care, end domestic violence, and improve education. Most important, women must remember the arduous struggle for suffrage and not fail to exercise their right to vote.

I would like you to take your minds back a 150 years. Imagine if you will that you are Charlotte Woodward, a nineteen-year-old glove maker working and living in Waterloo. Every day you sit for hours sewing gloves together, working for small wages you cannot even keep, with no hope of going on in school or owning property, knowing that if you marry, your children and even the clothes on your body will belong to your husband.

But then one day in July, 1848, you hear about a women's rights convention to be held in nearby Seneca Falls. It's a convention to discuss the social, civil, and religious conditions and rights of women. You run from house to house and you find other women who have heard the same news. Some are excited, others are amused or even shocked, and a few agree to come with you, for at least the first day.

When that day comes, July 19, 1848, you leave early in the morning in your horse-drawn wagon. You fear that no one else will come; and at first the road is empty, except for you and your neighbors. But suddenly, as you reach a crossroad, you see a few more wagons and carriages, then more and more, all going towards Wesleyan Chapel. Eventually you join the others to form one long procession on the road to equality.

Who were the others traveling that road to equality, traveling to that convention? Frederick Douglass, the former slave and great abolitionist, was on his way there and he described the participants as "few in numbers, moderate in resources, and very little known in the world. The most we had to connect us was a firm commitment that we were in the right and a firm faith that the right must ultimately prevail." In the wagons and carriages, on foot or horseback, were women like Rhoda Palmer. Seventy years later in 1918, at the age of 102, she would cast her first ballot in a New York State election.

Also traveling down that road to equality was Susan Quinn, who at fifteen will become the youngest signer of the Declaration of Sentiments. Catharine F. Stebbins, a veteran of activism starting when she was only twelve going door to door collecting anti-slavery petitions. She also, by the way, kept an anti-tobacco pledge on the parlor table and asked all her young male friends to sign up. She was a woman truly ahead of her time, as all the participants were.

I often wonder, when reflecting back on the Seneca Falls Convention, who of us—men and women—would have left our homes, our families, our work to make that journey 150 years ago. Think about the incredible courage it must have taken to join that procession. Ordinary men and women, mothers and fathers, sisters and brothers, husbands and wives, friends and neighbors. And just like those who have embarked on other journeys throughout American history, seeking freedom or escaping religious or political persecution, speaking out against slavery, working for labor rights. These men and women were motivated by dreams of better lives and more just societies.

At the end of the two-day convention, one hundred people, sixty-eight women and thirty-two men, signed the Declaration of Sentiments that you can now read on the wall at Wesleyan Chapel. Among the signers were some of the names we remember today: Elizabeth Cady Stanton and Lucretia Mott, Martha Wright and Frederick Douglass, and young Charlotte Woodward. The "Seneca Falls 100," as I like to call them, shared the radical idea that America fell far short of her ideals stated in our founding documents, denying citizenship to women and slaves.

Elizabeth Cady Stanton, who is frequently credited with

originating the idea for the Convention, knew that women were not only denied legal citizenship, but that society's cultural values and social structures conspired to assign women only one occupation and role, that of wife and mother. Of course, the reality was always far different. Women have always worked, and worked both in the home and outside the home for as long as history can record. And even though Stanton herself had a comfortable life and valued deeply her husband and seven children, she knew that she and all other women were not truly free if they could not keep wages they earned, divorce an abusive husband, own property, or vote for the political leaders who governed them. Stanton was inspired, along with the others who met, to rewrite our Declaration of Independence, and they boldly asserted, "We hold these truths to be self-evident, that all men and women are created equal."

The Shout Heard Around the World

"All men and all women." It was the shout heard around the world, and if we listen, we can still hear its echoes today. We can hear it in the voices of women demanding their full civil and political rights anywhere in the world. I've heard such voices and their echoes from women, around the world, from Belfast to Bosnia to Beijing, as they work to change the conditions for women and girls and improve their lives and the lives of their families. We can even hear those echoes today in Seneca Falls. We come together this time not by carriage, but by car or plane, by train or foot, and yes, in my case, by bus. We come together not to hold a convention, but to celebrate those who met here 150 years ago, to commemorate how far we have traveled since then, and to challenge ourselves to persevere on the journey that was begun all those many years ago.

We are, as one can see looking around this great crowd, men and women, old and young, different races, different backgrounds. We come to honor the past and imagine the future. That is the theme the President and I have chosen for the White House Millennium Council's efforts to remind and inspire Americans as we approach the year 2000. This is my last stop

Hillary Rodham Clinton

on the Millennium Council's Tour to Save America's Treasures—those buildings, monuments, papers and sites—that define who we are as a nation. They include not only famous symbols like the Star Spangled Banner and not only great political leaders like George Washington's revolutionary headquarters, or creative inventors like Thomas Edison's invention factory, but they include also the women of America who wrote our nation's past and must write its future.

Women like the ones we honor here—and, in fact, at the end of my tour yesterday, I learned that I was following literally in the footsteps of one of them, Lucretia Mott, who, on her way to Seneca Falls, stopped in Auburn to visit former slaves and went on to the Seneca Nations to meet with clan mothers, as I did.

Last evening, I visited the home of Mary Ann and Thomas McClintock in Waterloo, where the Declaration of Sentiments was drafted, and which the Park Service is planning to restore for visitors if the money needed can be raised. I certainly hope I can return here sometime in the next few years to visit that restoration.

Because we must tell and retell, learn and relearn these women's stories, and we must make it our personal mission, in our everyday lives, to pass these stories on to our daughters and sons. Because we cannot—we must not—ever forget that the rights and opportunities that we enjoy as women today were not just bestowed upon us by some benevolent ruler. They were fought for, agonized over, marched for, jailed for and even died for by brave and persistent women and men who came before us.

Every time we buy or sell or inherit property in our own name—let us thank the pioneers who agitated to change the laws that made that possible.

Every time, every time we vote, let us thank the women and men of Seneca Falls, Susan B. Anthony and all the others, who tirelessly crossed our nation and withstood ridicule and the rest to bring about the Nineteenth Amendment to the Constitution.

Every time we enter an occupation—a profession of our own choosing—and receive a paycheck that reflects earnings equal to a male colleague, let us thank the signers and women like Kate Mullaney,[1] whose house I visited yesterday, in Troy, New York.

Every time we elect a woman to office—let us thank groundbreaking leaders like Jeannette Rankin[2] and Margaret Chase Smith,[3] Hattie Caraway,[4] Louise Slaughter,[5] Bella Abzug,[6] Shirley Chisholm[7]—all of whom proved that a woman's place is truly in the House, and in the Senate, and one day, in the White House, as well.

And every time we take another step forward for justice in this nation—let us thank extraordinary women like Harriet Tubman, whose home in Auburn I visited yesterday, and who escaped herself from slavery, and then risked her life, time and again, to bring at least 200 other slaves to freedom as well.

We Must Keep Going

Harriet Tubman's rule for all of her underground railroad missions was to keep going. Once you started—no matter how scared you got, how dangerous it became—you were not allowed to turn back. That's a pretty good rule for life. It not only describes the women who gathered in Wesleyan Chapel in 1848, but it could serve as our own motto for today. We, too, cannot turn back. We, too, must keep going in our commitment to the dignity of every individual—to women's rights as human rights. We are on that road of the

1. An Irish laundress who established the first female labor union, the Collar Laundry Union, in the 1860s in Troy, New York.   2. The first female member of the House of Representatives (1917–1919 and 1941–1943), Jeanette Rankin was a committed suffragist and pacifist.   3. The first woman to be elected to both houses of Congress; in 1964, Smith became the first woman to have her name placed in nomination for the presidency by one of the two major political parties.   4. In 1932, Caraway became the first woman to be elected to the U.S. Senate.   5. Member of the House of Representatives since 1986 and considered by some to be "the most powerful woman in Congress."   6. Outspoken member of the House of Representatives during the 1970s, lawyer, and prominent women's rights activist.   7. The first black woman elected to the House of Representatives and the first to campaign for the presidency.

pioneers to Seneca Falls; they started down it 150 years ago. But now, we too, must keep going.

We may not face the criticism and derision they did. They understood that the Declaration of Sentiments would create no small amount of misconception, or misrepresentation and ridicule; they were called mannish women, old maids, fanatics, attacked personally by those who disagreed with them. One paper said, "These rights for women would bring a monstrous injury to all mankind." If it sounds familiar, it's the same thing that's always said when women keep going for true equality and justice.

Those who came here also understood that the Convention and the Declaration were only first steps down that road. What matters most is what happens when everyone packs up and goes back to their families and communities. What matters is whether sentiment and resolutions, once made, are fulfilled or forgotten. The Seneca Falls 100 pledged themselves to petition, and lit the pulpit and used every instrumentality within their power to affect their subjects. And they did. But they also knew they were not acting primarily for themselves. They knew they probably would not even see the changes they advocated in their own lifetime. In fact, only Charlotte Woodward lived long enough to see American women finally win the right to vote.

Those who signed that Declaration were doing it for the girls and women—for us—those of us in the twentieth century.

Elizabeth Cady Stanton wrote a letter to her daughters later in life enclosing a special gift and explaining why. "Dear Maggie and Hattie, this is my first speech," she wrote; "it contains all I knew at that time; I give this manuscript to my precious daughters in the hopes that they will finish the work that I have begun." And they have. Her daughter, Harriot Blatch, was the chief strategist of the suffrage movement in New York. Harriot's daughter, Nora Barney, was one of the first women to be a civil engineer. Nora's daughter, Rhoda Jenkins, became an architect. Rhoda's daughter, Colleen Jenkins-Sahlin, is an elected official in Greenwich, Connecticut. And her daughter, Elizabeth, is a thirteen-year-old who wrote about the six generations of Stantons in a book called *33 Things Every Girl Should Know.*

So, far into the twentieth century, the work is still being done; the journey goes on. Now, some might say that the only purpose of this celebration is to honor the past, that the work begun here is finished in America, that young women no longer face legal obstacles to whatever education or employment choices they choose to pursue. And I certainly believe and hope all of you agree that we should, every day, count our blessings as American women.

I know how much change I have seen in my own life. When I was growing up back in the fifties and sixties, there were still barriers that Mrs. Stanton would have recognized—scholarships I couldn't apply for, schools I couldn't go to, jobs I couldn't have—just because of my sex. Thanks to federal laws like the Civil Rights Act of 1964 and Title IX, and the Equal Pay Act, legal barriers to equality have fallen.

But if all we do is honor the past, then I believe we will miss the central point of the Declaration of Sentiments, which was, above all, a document about the future. The drafters of the Declaration imagined a different future for women and men, in a society based on equality and mutual respect. It falls to every generation to imagine the future, and it is our task to do so now.

We know, just as the women 150 years ago knew, that what we imagine will be principally for our daughters and sons in the twenty-first century. Because the work of the Seneca Falls Convention is just like the work of the nation itself—it's never finished, so long as there remain gaps between our ideals and reality. That is one of the great joys and beauties of the American experiment. We are always striving to build and move toward a more perfect union, that we on every occasion keep faith with our founding ideals, and translate them into reality. So what kind of future can we imagine together?

Imagining the Future

If we are to finish the work begun here—then no American should ever again face discrimination on the basis of gender, race, or sexual orientation anywhere in our country.

If we are to finish the work begun here—then $0.76 in a woman's paycheck for every dollar in a man's is still not enough. Equal pay for equal work can once and for all be achieved.

If we are to finish the work begun here—then families need more help to balance their responsibilities at work and at home. In a letter to Susan B. Anthony, Elizabeth Cady Stanton writes, "Come here and I will do what I can to help you with your address, if you will hold the baby and make the pudding." Even then, women knew we had to have help with child care. All families should have access to safe, affordable, quality child care.

If we are to finish the work begun here—then women and children must be protected against what the Declaration called the "chastisement of women," namely domestic abuse and violence. We must take all steps necessary to end the scourge of violence against women and punish the perpetrator. And our country must join the rest of the world, as so eloquently Secretary Albright[8] called for on Saturday night here in Seneca Falls, "Join the rest of the world and ratify the Convention on the Elimination of Discrimination Against Women."

If we are to finish the work begun here—we must do more than talk about family values; we must adopt policies that truly value families—policies like a universal system of health care insurance that guarantees every American's access to affordable, quality health care. Policies like taking all steps necessary to keep guns out of the hands of children and criminals. Policies like doing all that is necessary at all levels of our society to ensure high quality public education for every boy or girl no matter where that child lives.

If we are to finish the work begun here—we must ensure that women and men who work full-time earn a wage that lifts them out of poverty and all workers who retire have financial security in their later years through guaranteed Social Security and pensions.

If we are to finish the work begun here—we must be vigilant against the messages of a media-driven consumer culture that convinces our sons and daughters that what brand of sneakers they wear or cosmetics they use is more important than what they think, feel, know, or do.

8. Madeleine Albright, U.S. secretary of state (1996–2001).

And if we are to finish the work begun here—we must, above all else, take seriously the power of the vote and use it to make our voices heard. What the champions of suffrage understood was that the vote is not just a symbol of our equality, but that it can be, if used, a guarantee of results. It is the way we express our political views. It is the way we hold our leaders and governments accountable. It is the way we bridge the gap between what we want our nation to be and what it is.

But when will the majority of women voters of our country exercise their most fundamental political right? Can you imagine what any of the Declaration signers would say if they learned how many women fail to vote in elections? They would be amazed and outraged. They would agree with a poster I saw in 1996. On it, there is a picture of a woman with a piece of tape covering her mouth and under it, it says, "Most politicians think women should be seen and not heard. In the last election, 54 million women agreed with them."

One hundred and fifty years ago, the women at Seneca Falls were silenced by someone else. Today, women, we silence ourselves. We have a choice. We have a voice. And if we are going to finish the work begun here we must exercise our right to vote in every election we are eligible to vote in.

Much of who women are and what women do today can be traced to the courage, vision, and dedication of the pioneers who came together at Seneca Falls. Now it is our responsibility to finish the work they began. Let's ask ourselves, at the 200th anniversary of Seneca Falls, will they say that today's gathering also was a catalyst for action? Will they say that businesses, labor, religious organizations, the media, foundations, educators, every citizen in our society came to see the unfinished struggle of today as their struggle?

Will they say that we joined across lines of race and class, that we raised up those too often pushed down, and ultimately found strength in each other's differences and are resolved in our common cause? Will we, like the champions at Seneca Falls, recognize that men must play a central role in this fight? How can we ever forget the impassioned plea of Frederick Douglass, issued in our defense of the right to vote? How can we ever forget that young legislator from Tennessee by the name of Harry Burns, who was the deciding vote in ratifying the Nineteenth Amendment. He was planning on voting "no," but then he got a letter from his mother with a simple message. The letter said, "Be a good boy Harry and do the right thing." And he did! Tennessee became the last state to ratify, proving that you can never, ever overestimate the power of one person to alter the course of history, or the power of a little motherly advice.

Will we look back and see that we have finally joined the rest of the advanced economies by creating systems of education, employment, child care, and health care that support and strengthen families and give all women real choices in their lives?

At the 200th anniversary celebration, will they say that women today supported each other in the choices we make? Will we admit once and for all there is no single cookie-cutter model for being a successful and fulfilled woman today, that we have so many choices? We can choose full-time motherhood or no family at all or, like most of us, seek to strike a balance between our family and our work, always trying to do what is right in our lives. Will we leave our children a world where it is self-evident that all men and women, boys and girls are created equal? These are some of the questions we can ask ourselves.

Help us imagine a future that keeps faith with the sentiments expressed here in 1848. The future, like the past and the present, will not and cannot be perfect. Our daughters and granddaughters will face new challenges which we today cannot even imagine. But each of us can help prepare for that future by doing what we can to speak out for justice and equality, for women's rights and human rights, to be on the right side of history, no matter the risk or cost, knowing that eventually the sentiments we express and the causes we advocate will succeed because they are rooted in the conviction that all people are entitled by their creator and by the promise of America to the freedom, rights, responsibilities, and opportunity of full citizenship. That is what I imagine for the future. I invite you to imagine with me and then to work together to make that future a reality.

Thank you all very much.

Appendix of Biographies

Bella S. Abzug

The daughter of poor Russian immigrants, Bella S. Abzug was born and raised in the Bronx. In 1942 she graduated from Hunter College, where she was student body president, and went on to attend Columbia Law School on scholarship. At the time, she was one of a minute number of women law students across the country. After obtaining her law degree, Abzug practiced law privately for more than twenty years while raising two daughters with her husband. During the 1960s, she helped found Women Strike for Peace, a nationwide organization opposed to nuclear testing. She was also a stalwart critic of the Vietnam War.

In 1970, at the age of fifty, Abzug won a seat in the U.S. House of Representatives as a Democrat representing Manhattan. One of only twelve women in the House, Abzug quickly became a visible national figure, as well known for her feisty personality and flamboyant wide-brimmed hats as for her strong antiwar convictions. During three terms in Congress, from 1970 to 1976, Abzug was an indefatigable champion of social and economic justice. She cofounded the National Women's Political Caucus in 1971 and authored several bills intended to improve the status of women. She also helped to create the "Government in the Sunshine" law, which gave the public greater access to government records.

In 1976, Abzug gave up her congressional seat to seek the Democratic Party nomination for U.S. Senate. She narrowly lost the race to Daniel Patrick Moynihan, and later lost bids for New York City mayor in 1977 and Congress in 1978—losses that analysts attribute to her confrontational image and a conservative electorate. Abzug then served as the head of President Jimmy Carter's National Advisory Committee on Women until she was fired for issuing a report that criticized the administration's decision to cut funding for women's programs.

Abzug returned to practicing law in 1979, but remained in the public eye as a lecturer, television news commentator, and magazine columnist. She was also the founder of Women USA, a grassroots political action committee; an executive for the Women's Foreign Policy Council; and a major organizer of UN International Women's Conferences. In 1984, she coauthored the book *Gender Gap: Abzug's Guide to Political Power for Women*, in which she examined the causes of the "gender gap," the tendency of men and women to vote differently.

In her later years, Abzug became active in the environmental movement and cofounded the Women's Environment and Development Organization. She was considered an influential activist on global issues such as environmental security, economic justice, and women's empowerment. Abzug worked tenaciously for these causes until her death following heart surgery in 1998. Feminist Gloria Steinem said of Abzug that "in a just country, she would have been president."

Kathie Amatniek

Nothing is known of Kathie Amatniek except that she was a frequent participant in women's liberation and peace rallies during the late 1960s. She wrote and delivered the speech "A Funeral Oration for the Burial of Traditional Womanhood" in January 1968.

Susan B. Anthony

The most famous and devoted of all suffragists, Susan B. Anthony's early life was relatively inauspicious. She was born in 1820 in Massachusetts to Lucy Read and Daniel Anthony, a prosperous miller until the financial crisis of 1837. After the closing of the family's mill, Susan supported her family with the meager wages she earned as a teacher. She taught for ten years in district schools and private academies, receiving lower pay than men for the same work.

Anthony quit teaching in 1849, at the age of twenty-nine, to run her father's farm in New York. There she began to give lectures on women's rights and form friendships with famous abolitionist leaders such as Frederick Douglass and Amy Post. In 1851, she met Elizabeth Cady Stanton, in whom she found a kindred spirit. Challenging the all-male nature of the temperance movement, Anthony and Stanton formed the Women's New York State Temperance Society, which advocated women's right to vote on the issue of temperance and to divorce husbands who were drunks.

Together, Anthony and Stanton made New York State a mecca of women's rights activism. They promoted equal educational opportunities for women, less restrictive forms of clothing for women (referred to as "bloomers"), property rights for married women, and more liberal divorce laws. Anthony and Stanton were a well-matched team; Stanton was the intellectual mastermind and Anthony, whose unmarried status allowed her greater freedom and flexibility than Stanton, was the organizer and traveler. Anthony's aggressiveness in mobilizing support for women's rights led William

Henry Channing to call her the movement's Napoléon. By 1855, Anthony had lectured in every one of New York State's sixty-two counties.

When the Civil War began, women's rights advocates shifted their energies to the cause of abolition, and Anthony circulated a national petition urging Congress to abolish slavery with a constitutional amendment—her first appearance on the national scene. After the war's end, Anthony and Stanton lobbied for a constitutional amendment to guarantee voting rights for all citizens. They became convinced of the necessity of a separate movement that would focus exclusively on women's suffrage and would insist on federal protection of the voting rights of all citizens. To this end, they formed the National Woman Suffrage Association in 1869.

In 1872, Anthony and a group of other women cast ballots in the presidential election of 1872. She was arrested, convicted by a judge, and fined. Anthony refused to pay the fine. Her persuasive speech on the injustice of her arrest revived support for a constitutional amendment for women's suffrage. Such an amendment reached the Senate floor in 1876 but was resoundingly defeated. Regardless, Anthony continued a busy lecture circuit advocating women's suffrage; her industriousness made her a national celebrity. Unfortunately, Anthony died in 1906, fourteen years before suffrage was finally achieved.

Anthony's legacy is preserved by hundreds of interviews that she gave to local newspapers; four volumes of the *History of Women's Suffrage*, coauthored with Elizabeth Cady Stanton, Matilda Joslyn Gage, and Ida Husted Harper; and her many speeches, which remain strong testaments to her achievements. Her greatest legacy, however, is the Nineteenth Amendment, which is commonly referred to as the "Susan B. Anthony amendment."

Benazir Bhutto

Benazir Bhutto was born in Karachi, Pakistan, to a landowning, politically prominent family. Her father, Zulfikar Ali Bhutto, often served in government posts away from home. Benazir was tutored by an English governess until the age of sixteen, when she traveled to the United States to attend Harvard's Radcliffe College. She received a degree in government in 1973, then studied politics, philosophy, and economics at Oxford University in England.

In 1977, Bhutto's father, who had been elected prime minister of Pakistan, was ousted from power by a military regime that charged that the elections had been fixed. The regime imprisoned Zulfikar Ali Bhutto in 1977 for conspiring to murder a party colleague; two years later, he was hanged by the military government led by General Zia Ul-Haq.

Benazir, who had returned to Pakistan shortly before her father's arrest, was arrested repeatedly by the military regime between 1977 and 1984. When the regime finally allowed her to leave Pakistan in 1984, she went to live in London. She returned a year later to attend the funeral of her brother, a member of the resistance who died under mysterious circumstances. While in Pakistan, Bhutto took part in antigovernment rallies and again was arrested.

In April 1986, bolstered by tremendous public support, Bhutto demanded that General Zia step down from his post. The following month she and her mother were elected as cochairs of the Pakistan People's Party. She was arrested again, but soon released.

Bhutto was elected prime minister of Pakistan in 1988, thereby becoming the first woman to lead an Islamic nation. She intended to return the country to civilian rule, but was dismissed from office two years later by Pakistan President Ghulam Ishaq Khan. She ran again for prime minister in 1993 and was reelected.

Bhutto was again dismissed from office in 1996 following allegations of corruption and mismanagement. Bhutto's husband was also criticized for supposedly taking bribes.

During her time as prime minister, Bhutto supported a leftist platform; she strove to help the disadvantaged obtain jobs, health care, education, food, and a living wage. She was also adamant in her belief that Islamic countries must improve their treatment of women. Bhutto is the author of *Foreign Policy in Perspective* and *Daughter of Destiny*, and the recipient of the 1988 Bruno Kreisky Award for Human Rights.

Charlotte Bunch

Charlotte Bunch graduated magna cum laude from Duke University with a bachelor's degree in history and political science in 1966. She then did graduate research on educational and social change at the Institute for Policy Studies in Washington, D.C.

In 1974, Bunch created *Quest: A Feminist Journal*, considered one of the first journals to promote political change as a method to improve women's status in society. During the 1970s and 1980s, Bunch earned nationwide attention as a feminist writer and lesbian activist. Her many books include *Class and Feminism*, *Lesbianism and the Women's Movement*, *Learning Our Way: Essays in Feminist Education*, and *International Feminism: Networking Against Female Sexual Slavery*.

Bunch was particularly active in the arena of international feminism. In 1989 she founded the Center for Women's Global Leadership at Douglass College, Rutgers University, to promote the leadership of women and advance feminist perspectives in policy making around the world. At the 1993 UN Conference on Human Rights held in Vienna, Bunch called for international attention to women's issues. Her advocacy was largely responsible for the inclusion of gender and sexual orientation on the global human rights agenda.

In 1996, Bunch was inducted into the Women's Hall of Fame for her efforts in support of women's human rights. She is now a professor at Rutgers University, where she continues to act as director of the Center for Women's Global Leadership.

Shirley Chisholm

Shirley Anita St. Hill Chisholm was born in 1924 in Brooklyn. Her father and mother, West Indian immigrants who barely subsisted on their meager incomes as a factory worker and a housecleaner, respectively, sent Shirley and her sisters to the island of Barbados to be reared by their maternal grandmother. There Shirley received an excellent education in Barbados's British school system; when she returned to Brooklyn at the age of ten, she was considered a superior student.

At Brooklyn College, Chisholm was a member of the debating society—which shaped her shrewd oratory style—as well as a volunteer for the National Urban League and the National Association for the Advancement of Colored People. After graduating from college, Chisholm earned a master's degree in child education and simultaneously taught at a Harlem nursing school. Later, she became the supervisor of the largest nursery school network in New York.

In 1964, Chisholm won a seat in the New York State Assembly in a landslide victory. As a member of the assembly, she instituted a program to provide college funding to disadvantaged youths and introduced a bill that secured unemployment insurance for domestic workers and day-care providers.

Four years after her initial foray into politics, Chisholm won a seat in the U.S. House of Representatives, becoming the first African American woman elected to Congress. During her campaign, she described herself as "unbossed and unbought" and promised to "vote no on every money bill that . . . provides any funds for the department of defense." Chisholm used her widely respected oratory skills to further the causes of the disadvantaged, especially children. She was an advocate for the rights of African

Americans, other minorities, and women; an opponent of the Vietnam War; and a supporter of pro-labor policies such as a higher minimum wage.

In 1972, Chisholm became the first African American woman to campaign for the presidency. She maintained that her attempt, although unsuccessful, would help other women "feel themselves as capable of running for high political office as any wealthy, good-looking white male."

Chisholm retired from Congress in 1982 and has since remained active in politics, education, and women's rights. A teacher at various universities, she cofounded and currently chairs the National Political Congress of Black Women. She has also served on the Advisory Council of the National Organization for Women.

Hillary Rodham Clinton

Hillary Diane Rodham was born in Chicago, Illinois, in 1947, and grew up in the suburb of Park Ridge. In 1969 she graduated from Wellesley College and then enrolled in Yale Law School, where she met fellow law student Bill Clinton. The couple married in 1975; their only child, Chelsea, was born in 1980. Hillary worked as a high-powered attorney in Little Rock, Arkansas, while her husband served for twelve years as governor of the state. In recognition of her advocacy work for children and families, she was named Arkansas Woman of the Year in 1984. In 1991, she was named by the *National Law Journal* as one of the one hundred most influential lawyers in America.

Upon her husband's election to the presidency in 1992, Clinton became extremely active in government affairs, with health care as her greatest priority. In 1993, Clinton led the National Task Force on Health Care at the request of the president. Although her attempt to reform the health care industry to provide coverage for all Americans failed, she continues to be a forceful ally of Americans who lack health insurance. She has worked for increased immunizations for preschool-age children, expanded health insurance coverage for children, and innovative prenatal care.

In 1996, Clinton published her book *It Takes a Village and Other Lessons Children Teach Us*, in which she argues that society must take responsibility for raising children. A frequent host of conferences on children's issues, Clinton took a leading role in developing President Clinton's child-care initiative, which would provide government resources for child care. She is also a proponent of an improved foster care system. In addition to her work for health care and children's issues, Clinton is also a vocal advocate for human rights and the economic empowerment of women across the globe, addressing these issues as a speaker in Europe, Asia, Latin America, and Africa.

In 2000, Clinton moved to New York to campaign for the U.S. Senate seat vacated by retiring Daniel Patrick Moynihan, a decision that prompted considerable controversy, in part because of her husband's impeachment as president. She won the most highly publicized Senate battle in U.S history and became the first First Lady to be elected senator.

Angela Y. Davis

The daughter of two teachers, Angela Yvonne Davis was born in 1944 in Birmingham, Alabama, at the time a hotbed of racism and social unrest. Davis's parents had many communist friends, and Davis herself joined a communist youth group at a young age. She studied abroad at the Frankfurt School in Germany and at the University of Paris; later she attended Brandeis University in Massachusetts and graduated magna cum laude.

As a doctoral candidate in philosophy at the University of California at San Diego in the late 1960s, Davis became a member of the Communist Party and the Black Panthers, a group of black revolutionaries who were committed to fighting racism. Because of her association with these radical groups, Davis was watched closely by the U.S. government. Also as a result of these associations, the University of California at Los Angeles dismissed her in 1970 from her position as lecturer in philosophy despite her excellent teaching record.

That same year, Davis was charged with conspiring to free black revolutionary George Jackson in a shoot-out in Marin County, California. She became the third woman to appear on the FBI's most wanted list. Davis evaded the police for two weeks, during which time signs appeared all over the country announcing, "Angela, sister, you are welcome in this house." Davis was finally discovered in New York City and arrested. She spent sixteen months in prison before she was acquitted of all charges by an all-white jury.

After her release from prison in 1971, Davis published a collection of her essays, entitled *If They Come in the Morning: Voices of Resistance*; in this book she explains her belief in communist theory and discusses racial oppression in the United States. She is also the author of *Angela Davis: An Autobiography*, published in 1974, and *Women, Race, and Class*, published in 1981. The latter book quickly became a feminist classic for its exploration of the relationship between sexism, racism, and classism. Davis is currently a tenured professor at the University of California at Santa Cruz; a committed political activist; and a frequent lecturer on politics, race, and women's rights.

Serrin M. Foster

Serrin M. Foster is the president of Feminists for Life of America (FFLA), an organization whose mission is to help pregnant women find alternatives to abortion. As FFLA president, Foster travels to universities across the country speaking about why the pro-life position is a feminist one. She serves on the advisory boards of the Ivy League Coalition for Life and American Collegians for Life.

Betty Friedan

As author of *The Feminine Mystique*, her 1963 examination of the dissatisfaction of American suburban housewives, Betty Friedan is considered the founder of the women's liberation movement. Her book, which quickly became an international best-seller, was the first piece of writing to articulate women's frustrations with their societal roles as housewives.

Like most middle-class women of her generation, Friedan married and became a housewife after her graduation from Smith College in 1942. However, she was deeply unhappy with her daily routine of cleaning, cooking, and child care. Wondering whether she was alone in these feelings, she sent a questionnaire to other Smith alumnae. Their responses, which revealed similar discontent, became the basis of *The Feminine Mystique*. In the book, Friedan argued that society "does not permit women to accept or gratify their basic need to grow and fulfill their potentialities as human beings."

Not long after the book was published, Friedan founded the National Organization for Women and acted as the organization's president. NOW was the first organization to argue for antidiscrimination laws in the workplace—one of the greatest achievements of the women's liberation movement. Since the 1960s, Friedan has been a leading advocate for women's rights as a social activist, writer, and lecturer. Her most recent book is *The Second Stage*, in which she details contemporary feminism's newest challenges.

Frances D. Gage

Frances Dana Barker, born and raised on a farm in Union Township, Ohio, in 1808, was frustrated at an early age by the limited roles of girls and women. When she was ten, her father admonished her for helping a worker on the farm to make a barrel, remarking, "What a pity she was not a boy!" She later wrote about this episode, "Then and there sprang up my hatred to the limitations of sex. . . . I was outspoken forever afterward."

Her outspokenness soon found an outlet in the abolition, temperance, and women's rights movements. While raising eight children with her husband, James L. Gage, Frances Gage wrote letters and articles championing these causes. She became a regular contributor to two women's rights newspapers: *Lily*, edited by Amelia Bloomer, and the *Saturday Visiter*. One of the most vocal supporters of the women's rights movement in Ohio, Gage drafted a petition to the state legislature in 1850 urging that the words "white" and "male" be stricken from the constitution. She presided over the second Ohio women's rights convention, held in Akron in 1851, in which she allowed the African American activist Sojourner Truth to speak despite protestations from members of the audience. She also led the third national women's rights convention, held in Cleveland in 1853.

During the Civil War, Gage stopped her work as an editor of the *Ohio Cultivator* and *Field Notes*, two farmers' weekly papers, to assist the abolition movement. She served for thirteen months as the superintendent of a camp of five hundred freed slaves on Parris Island, South Carolina, then returned to the North, where she delivered lectures publicizing the plight of freedpeople, the proceeds of which went to support former slaves and soldiers. She also led efforts to provide aid to soldiers. Undeterred by a severe accident in which her carriage overturned, Gage remained a fervent speaker on women's rights, abolitionism, and temperance until her death by paralysis in 1884.

Kate Michelman

Like other women who grew up during the 1950s, Kate Michelman's main hope was to find a husband and have children. By 1970, she had achieved this goal; she was married to a college professor, with whom she had three daughters. However, when her children were still young, her husband abruptly left her.

Weeks afterward, Michelman learned that she was pregnant. Feeling unable to provide financial and emotional support for another child, she sought an abortion. However, because abortion was severely restricted at that time, Michelman had to convince a hospital panel of all-male doctors that she was not capable of raising another child. The panel finally agreed to allow her an abortion, but required that she obtain written permission from her husband.

Michelman's difficulty in obtaining an abortion spurred her to prochoice activism. Shortly after the 1973 Supreme Court decision in *Roe v. Wade* legalized abortion, she became a forceful proponent of abortion rights. She has been the president of the National Abortion and Reproductive Rights League since 1985 and has also served as the executive director of Planned Parenthood in Harrisburg, Pennsylvania.

Lucretia Mott

Lucretia Coffin, born in 1793 on Nantucket Island, Massachusetts, was raised in a family of devoted Quakers. The Quaker religion, which supports the equality of men and women, shaped many of Lucretia's beliefs. She boarded at a Quaker school in New York, called Nine Partners, where she became a "Hicksite," a follower of Elias Hicks, a passionate Quaker abolitionist. At Nine Partners she also met teacher James Mott, whom she married in 1811; they had six children.

The speeches Lucretia gave at Quaker meetings were so powerful that the church eventually recognized her as a minister. She preached throughout the Northeast, encouraging Quakers to boycott products created with slave labor, a practice that she and her husband had followed for years. Having been excluded from formally organized abolitionist groups because she was a woman, she founded the Philadelphia Female Anti-Slavery Society in 1833. Four years later, speaking at the First Anti-Slavery Convention of American Women in New York City, Mott became the first activist to articulate the connection between the anti-slavery movement and the cause of women's rights. In 1840, she was named a delegate from Pennsylvania to the World's Anti-Slavery Convention in London, but could attend only as a visitor because the convention barred women from serving as delegates.

At the convention's end, she and Elizabeth Cady Stanton resolved to call a convention to address the question of women's rights, a goal that would be fulfilled eight years later in Seneca Falls, New York. Mott, a fiery speaker, drew crowds to early women's rights conventions.

Although Mott was a devout abolitionist who participated in slave rescues, as a pacifist she was horrified by the outbreak of the Civil War and rejoiced when the war ended. Shortly afterward, she became embroiled in the conflict over whether the Fourteenth Amendment, which gave black men the right to vote, should be expanded to include women. Mott, who supported the right of both sexes and all races to vote, joined forces with Elizabeth Cady Stanton and Susan B. Anthony to promote a constitutional amendment for women's suffrage.

Mott traveled the country to speak on women's rights and various other causes until her death at the age of eighty-seven. Her strong belief in the equality of all Americans, including African Americans, Native Americans, and women, made her one of the most radical feminist reformers of her time.

Emmeline Pankhurst

Emmeline Pankhurst was born in Manchester, England, in 1858, the daughter of Robert Goulden, a successful businessman who campaigned against slavery, and Sophia Crane, an ardent feminist. Emmeline was taken to women's suffrage meetings by her mother starting in the early 1870s. After her education at a finishing school in Paris, Emmeline married Richard Pankhurst, a lawyer, socialist, and advocate of women's suffrage, who was twenty-four years her senior. The two helped form the Women's Franchise League, a women's suffrage group, and were active members of the liberal Independent Labour Party.

After her husband's death in 1898, Pankhurst remained active in English politics. Dissatisfied with existing women's political organizations, she founded the Women's Social and Political Union, whose primary goal was to bolster support for suffrage among working-class women. The WSPU, frustrated by the media's lack of interest in women's voting rights, staged an attention-getting event. On October 13, 1905, Christabel Pankhurst, one of Emmeline's daughters, and Annie Kenney interrupted a government meeting, shouting, "Will the Liberal Government give votes to women?" Police attempted to evict them from the meeting but the two women refused to leave. Pankhurst and Kenney were arrested and charged with assault; they were found guilty and fined five shillings each. When the women refused to pay their fines, they were sent to prison. The tactic, which gave WSPU feminists the name "militants," shocked the nation.

Emmeline Pankhurst was one of the most active instigators of civil disobedience as a method to obtain women's suffrage. She was jailed repeatedly and endured numerous hunger strikes. Later in life, Pankhurst abandoned her socialist beliefs and became a member of the Conservative Party in Britain, a decision that caused great discord within her family.

Ernestine Potowski Rose

Ernestine Louise Siismondi Potowski, the daughter of an Orthodox rabbi, was born in Poland in 1810. She received an extensive education in Hebrew and the Jewish Scriptures—which was uncommon for girls at that time—but rejected Judaism as an adolescent because she felt the religion treated women poorly. At the age of sixteen, Ernestine inherited a large sum of money from her mother. Her father tried to use this money as a dowry, promising Ernestine's hand to a significantly older man, but Ernestine protested and argued her case successfully in a Polish court.

In 1827, she left Poland, traveling for some time before settling in England. There she befriended a variety of social reformers and philanthropists, including utopian socialist Robert Owen. In 1835, she and Owen formed the Association of All Classes of All Nations, an organization aimed at making the world "as happy as possible"; in 1843, she would help to found a utopian community in Skaneateles, New York.

At the age of twenty-six, Ernestine married William Emma Rose in England. They moved to New York City, where he worked as a silversmith and she created cologne. Rose also began to lobby for married women's property rights with Elizabeth Cady Stanton and Pauline Wright. She had several interests as a reformer: She was an activist for women's rights; a supporter of the freethought movement, a group of social reformers who demanded a complete separation of church and state; an advocate for temperance; and an abolitionist who worked with Frederick Douglass and William Lloyd Garrison. In the sphere of women's rights, she fought for universal suffrage, less restrictive divorce laws, and greater access to education for women. Her spirited lectures on these subjects, which she gave in more than twenty-three states, earned her the title of "Queen of the Platform."

Rose was praised for providing the women's rights movement with an intellectual foundation, but she was also attacked as a foreigner and an outspoken agnostic. Many in the suffrage movement felt that her radical views made her detrimental to the cause. Susan B. Anthony once stated that Rose, due to her belief in the separation of church and state and her conviction that divorce was often necessary, was too far ahead of her time to be properly understood and appreciated.

Phyllis Schlafly

Phyllis Schlafly received a bachelor's and a law degree from Washington University, and earned a master's in political science from Harvard University. She became a national leader of the conservative movement with the publication of her 1964 book *A Choice Not an Echo*. In 1972, she founded the still existing Eagle Forum, a national volunteer organization that supports conservative principles.

Schlafly, the mother of six children, was one of the most vocal opponents of the women's liberation movement of the 1960s and 1970s. She argued that radical feminism, by encouraging women to seek self-fulfillment above all else, degraded the institutions of marriage and motherhood upon which a moral society is founded. In her campaign against feminism, Schlafly appeared on college campuses more frequently than any other conservative.

During the 1980s, Schlafly worked as a lawyer and served as a member of the Reagan administration's Commission on the Bicentennial of the U.S. Constitution. During her tenure on this commission, Schlafly testified before more than fifty congressional and state legislative committees on issues related to the Constitution, national defense, and the family.

Today, Schlafly publishes a monthly newsletter, the *Phyllis Schlafly Report*, and a syndicated column that appears in more than one hundred newspapers. She is also a frequent radio commentator and the editor of several books.

Anna Howard Shaw

Born in England in 1847, Anna Howard Shaw spent her childhood with her mother and sisters in a rugged cabin on Michigan's frontier, while her father lived on the East Coast. The grueling responsibilities Anna shouldered as a child inspired her aggressive pursuit of education in hopes of a better life. After attending Albion College, she earned a diploma from the Boston University Theological School and was licensed as an Episcopal minister in 1878; however, because she was a woman, she was denied ordination until 1880.

While ministering in Earl Dennis, Massachusetts, Shaw earned her M.D. from Boston Medical School but was uninterested in pursuing a career in medicine. Instead, having discovered her talent as an orator, she began lecturing on temperance and women's suffrage throughout Massachusetts. Women's movement leaders, impressed by Shaw's charisma as a speaker, tried to attract her to their organizations. Ultimately, Shaw developed a loyalty to Susan B. Anthony, whose niece Lucy became Shaw's companion for life.

Anthony primed Shaw for her post as president of the National American Women's Suffrage Association in 1904. Unfortunately, Shaw was by most accounts an ineffective leader. She failed to recognize the need for a national women's suffrage strategy and denounced Alice Paul—who authored the first equal rights amendment—for designing such a strategy. When members began to encourage former NAWSA president Carrie Chapman Catt to return, Shaw resigned as president. After her resignation, Shaw continued to speak on the issue of women's suffrage. Her irreverent tone and often hilarious use of sarcasm won her popularity as a lecturer.

When the United States entered World War I, Shaw stopped her lecture tours to lead the Woman's Committee of the Council of National Defense, an organization that coordinated women's relief work in the war. She was awarded the Distinguished Service Medal by Congress in 1919 and died the same year of pneumonia.

Elizabeth Cady Stanton

Born in Johnstown, New York, in 1815, Elizabeth Cady was the daughter of Margaret Livingston and Daniel Cady, a distinguished lawyer, state assemblyman, and congressman. During her childhood, she absorbed legal principles from her father and received a formal education at Johnstown Academy and Emma Willard's Troy Female Seminary. In 1840 she married Henry Brewster Stanton, a well-known abolitionist who lent most of his money to the anti-slavery cause.

After her marriage, Elizabeth Cady Stanton became involved in the anti-slavery movement; however, as a woman, she was unwelcome at many abolitionist meetings. This injustice inspired her to organize a movement for women's rights. In 1848, years after she had initially conceived the idea, Stanton initiated the Seneca Falls Women's Rights Convention, the first known public meeting where women gathered to demand the legal rights that were denied to them. The convention established Stanton as one of the two most prominent figures, along with Susan B. Anthony, of the women's rights movement. Later, she became a founder and president of the New York Women's Temperance Society, a founder and president of the American Equal Rights Association, and president of the National American Woman Suffrage Association.

Stanton convened the American Equal Rights Association in the spring of 1866 to promote universal suffrage. At the time, Congress was considering new suffrage requirements to allow black men the right to vote. Increasingly frustrated by the refusal of abolitionist leaders to support universal suffrage, Stanton voiced her opposition to the Fifteenth Amendment, which would give the right to vote to black men—a view that she would later abandon but one that has tainted her image as a great supporter of human rights.

Throughout her life, Stanton was a prolific lecturer and writer on the topic of suffrage. Anthony, who unlike Stanton had no children and was unmarried, had the freedom to promote many of Stanton's ideas. As Stanton later wrote, "I forged the thunderbolts and she fired them." However, despite her role as president of the

National Women's Suffrage Association, Stanton increasingly felt alienated from the movement, whose newest adherents were members of evangelical churches. In the last decades of her life, she was an outspoken critic of churches on the grounds that Christian teachings degraded women. This view was reflected in her book *Women's Bible*, published in sections during the 1890s.

By the age of eighty, Stanton suffered serious health problems. She could barely stand due to weak knees, and her eyesight was severely diminished. However, she continued to advocate suffrage by dictating articles. She died at her home in New York in 1902, leaving an unmailed letter to Theodore Roosevelt asking for his endorsement of women's suffrage.

Gloria Steinem

After her parents' divorce in 1942, when she was eight, Gloria Steinem became the primary caregiver for her mother, who experienced debilitating bouts of depression. The two lived in Toledo, Ohio, in a shabby house without heat. However, Gloria was able to attend college on scholarship at Smith College, from which she graduated magna cum laude. She then won a fellowship to study for two years in India at the University of Delhi and the University of Calcutta. In India, she became involved in a nonviolent government protest and developed an interest in politics.

In 1960, back in the United States, Steinem began a career as a freelance journalist in New York City. Although she wanted to cover serious political issues, her male magazine editors suggested that she work undercover as a waitress in a New York Playboy Bunny Club and report on her experience. She later published an exposé of the club's low wages, poor working conditions, and rampant sexual harassment. The article was Steinem's first piece of strong investigative reporting, but it was rarely considered as such; many editors simply saw that she had worked as a Bunny and refused to treat her as a serious writer.

Regardless of this setback, Steinem eventually made headway as a respected political journalist. In 1968, she covered Senator George McGovern's presidential campaign, an assignment that landed her a position at *New York* magazine. As a columnist there, Steinem wrote on diverse political issues, including the assassination of Martin Luther King Jr. and United Farm Workers demonstrations led by Cesar Chavez.

Steinem also began to attend feminist meetings during the late 1960s. Eventually, she became one of the most articulate and charismatic leaders of the women's liberation movement. One of her central arguments was that feminist and civil rights movements were interdependent; her article explaining this idea, "After Black Power, Women's Liberation," won the Penney-Missouri Journalism Award.

Along with Bella Abzug, Shirley Chisholm, and Betty Friedan, Steinem formed the National Women's Political Caucus in 1971 to encourage women to participate in the 1972 presidential election. Steinem also called for the inclusion of a prochoice position in the Democratic platform. Around that time, she developed a friendship with Dorothy Pittman Hughes, an African American who founded one of the first community day-care centers in New York. In 1972 the two formed their own magazine, *Ms.*, to promote issues such as legalized abortion, equal pay for women, and the passage of the Equal Rights Amendment. Steinem is still a consulting editor of the magazine.

As the editor of *Ms.*, Steinem remained active in politics. In 1975 she helped plan the women's agenda for the Democratic National Convention, and in 1977 she participated in the National Conference of Women in Houston. She has also worked as an activist for political organizations such as the Coalition of Labor Union Women, Voters for Choice, and Women Against Pornography. An author of several books and a member of the Women's Hall of Fame, Steinem is one of the most prominent feminists living today.

Sojourner Truth

In 1799, Sojourner Truth was born as Isabella Baumfree in Hurley, New York, the daughter of James and Elizabeth, who were slaves. As a child, Isabella had a series of owners, but for most of her life she belonged to the John Dumont family. In 1815 she married another of Dumont's slaves, Thomas, with whom she had five children. In the year before her legal emancipation from slavery in 1827, she left the Dumont family of her own volition. Soon afterward, when a member of Dumont's wife's family sold Isabella's son into slavery in Alabama, Isabella went to court and sued successfully for her son's return.

She became a born-again Christian and moved to New York City, leaving her husband behind. Working at a private household she met Robert Matthews, otherwise known as the prophet Matthias, and joined his commune, which advocated spiritualism, temperance, and holistic health practices. In 1843, she changed her name to Sojourner Truth—meaning "itinerant preacher"—and traveled the East Coast preaching the word of Christ. She settled for a while in the Northampton Association in Massachusetts, a utopian community that supported the anti-slavery movement and women's rights. Later she was able to buy property of her own with the proceeds from a book that she dictated, *The Narrative of Sojourner Truth*.

Truth became known as a forceful and moving speaker on the topics of abolition, the rights of freed slaves, and the rights of women. She met with such famous abolitionists as Frederick Douglass, Harriet Beecher Stowe, and President Abraham Lincoln. In 1867, Truth led an effort to find freedpeople jobs in New York and Michigan; she also developed a plan to help freed slaves settle in government lands in the West. Although Truth was virtually unschooled, her sagacious manner of expression earned her respect above that of many well-educated lecturers.

Sarah Weddington

Sarah Weddington is best known for her role in the 1973 landmark Supreme Court decision *Roe v. Wade*. As a young attorney fresh out of law school, she successfully argued the case of Norma McCorvey—known as Jane Roe— at a time when the lawyer's lounge at the Supreme Court contained no facilities for women. The decision in that case mandated that abortion be legal within the first two trimesters of a woman's pregnancy. Weddington received a number of awards for her work on the case, including the Planned Parenthood Federal of America's Margaret Sanger Award.

In 1972, Weddington was elected to the first of three terms in the Texas House of Representatives. As a legislator, she helped reform Texas rape statutes, support the state's ratification of the Equal Rights Amendment, and prevent antiabortion legislation.

From 1978 to 1981, Weddington worked as an assistant to President Jimmy Carter. She led White House efforts to extend the time limit for ratification of the ERA. She also helped select women for federal judiciary appointments and implemented programs to assist the equal treatment of women.

Weddington is the recipient of several honorary degrees, as well as such awards as *Time* magazine's Outstanding Young American Leaders and the *Ladies' Home Journal*'s Woman of the Future. She is the author of the book *A Question of Choice*, in which she describes her experience in *Roe v. Wade*. Currently, Weddington works as a lawyer in Austin and is a senior lecturer at the University of Texas at Austin.

For Further Research

CHARLOTTE BUNCH AND ROXANNA CARILLO, *Gender Violence: A Development and Human Rights Issue*. Dublin: Attic Press, 1992.

CHARLOTTE BUNCH AND SANDRA POLLACK, EDS., *Learning Our Way: Essays in Feminist Education*. Trumansburg, NY: Crossing Press, 1983.

ELINOR BURKETT, *The Right Women: A Journey Through the Heart of Conservative America*. New York: Scribner, 1998.

PHYLLIS CHESLER, *Letters to a Young Feminist*. New York: Four Walls Eight Windows, 1997.

OLIVIA COOLIDGE, *Women's Rights: The Suffrage Movement in America, 1848–1920*. New York: Dutton, 1966.

DANIELLE CRITTENDEN, *What Our Mothers Didn't Tell Us: Why Happiness Eludes the Modern Woman*. New York: Simon & Schuster, 1999.

MARY DALY, *Quintessence—Realizing the Archaic Future: A Radical Elemental Feminist Manifesto*. Boston: Beacon Press, 1998.

ANGELA Y. DAVIS, *Women, Culture, and Politics*. New York: Random House, 1989.

———, *Women, Race, and Class*. New York: Random House, 1981.

TOM DIGBY, ED., *Men Doing Feminism*. New York: Routledge, 1998.

ANDREA DWORKIN, *Woman Hating*. New York: Dutton, 1974.

ALICE ECHOLS, *Daring to Be Bad: Radical Feminism in America, 1967–1975*. Minneapolis: University of Minnesota Press, 1989.

SARA M. EVANS, *Born for Liberty: A History of Women in America*. New York: Free Press, 1989.

DORIS FABER, *Petticoat Politics: How American Women Won the Right to Vote.* New York: Lothrop, Lee & Shepard, 1967.

SUSAN FALUDI, *Backlash: The Undeclared War Against American Women.* New York: Crown, 1991.

ELEANOR FLEXNER, *Century of Struggle: The Women's Rights Movement in the United States.* Cambridge, MA: Belknap Press, 1975.

ELIZABETH FOX-GENOVESE, *"Feminism Is Not the Story of My Life": How Today's Feminist Elite Has Lost Touch with the Real Concerns of Women.* New York: Anchor Books, 1996.

BETTY FRIEDAN, *It Changed My Life: Writings on the Women's Movement.* New York: Random House, 1976.

———, *The Feminine Mystique.* New York: W.W. Norton, 1963.

———, *The Second Stage.* New York: Summit Books, 1981.

F. CAROLYN GRAGLIA, *Domestic Tranquility: A Brief Against Feminism.* Dallas, TX: Spence, 1998.

GERMAINE GREER, *The Whole Woman.* New York: A.A. Knopf, 1999.

MIRIAM GURKO, *The Ladies of Seneca Falls: Birth of the Women's Rights Movement.* New York: Macmillan, 1974.

SHARON HAYS, *The Cultural Contradictions of Motherhood.* New Haven, CT: Yale University Press, 1996.

LESLIE HEYWOOD AND JENNIFER DRAKE, EDS., *Third Wave Agenda: Being Feminist, Doing Feminism.* Minneapolis: University of Minnesota Press, 1997.

WINSTON LANGLEY AND VIVIAN C. FOX, *Women's Rights in the United States: A Documentary History.* Westport, CT: Greenwood Press, 1994.

CHRISTOPHER LASCH, *Women and the Common Life: Love, Marriage, and Feminism.* New York: W.W. Norton, 1997.

KAREN LEHRMAN, *The Lipstick Proviso: Women, Sex, and Power in the Real World*. New York: Doubleday, 1997.

CATHARINE A. MACKINNON, *Toward a Feminist Theory of the State*. Cambridge, MA: Harvard University Press, 1989.

NAN BAUER MAGLIN AND DONNA PERRY, EDS., *"Bad Girls"/ "Good Girls": Women, Sex, and Power in the Nineties*. New Brunswick, NJ: Rutgers University Press, 1996.

NANCY MYRON AND CHARLOTTE BUNCH, *Lesbianism and the Women's Movement*. Baltimore: Diana Press, 1975.

KATIE ROIPHE, *The Morning After: Sex, Fear, and Feminism on Campus*. Boston: Little, Brown, 1993.

MIRIAM SCHNEIR, ED., *Feminism in Our Time: The Essential Writings, World War II to the Present*. New York: Vintage Books, 1994.

ELIZABETH CADY STANTON, *Eighty Years and More*. New York: Source Book Press, 1970.

ELIZABETH CADY STANTON, SUSAN B. ANTHONY, AND MATILDA JOSLYN GAGE, EDS., *History of Woman Suffrage*. Rochester, NY: Susan B. Anthony, 1887.

GLORIA STEINEM, *Moving Beyond Words*. New York: Simon & Schuster, 1994.

ROSALYN TERBORG-PENN, *African American Women in the Struggle for the Vote, 1850–1920*. Bloomington: Indiana University Press, 1998.

SHEILA TOBIAS, *Faces of Feminism: An Activist's Reflections on the Women's Movement*. Boulder, CO: Westview Press, 1997.

LISA TUTTLE, *Encyclopedia of Feminism*. New York: Facts On File, 1986.

REBECCA WALKER, ED., *To Be Real: Telling the Truth and Changing the Face of Feminism*. New York: Anchor Books, 1995.

NAOMI WOLF, *Promiscuities: The Secret Struggle for Womanhood*. New York: Random House, 1997.

Index